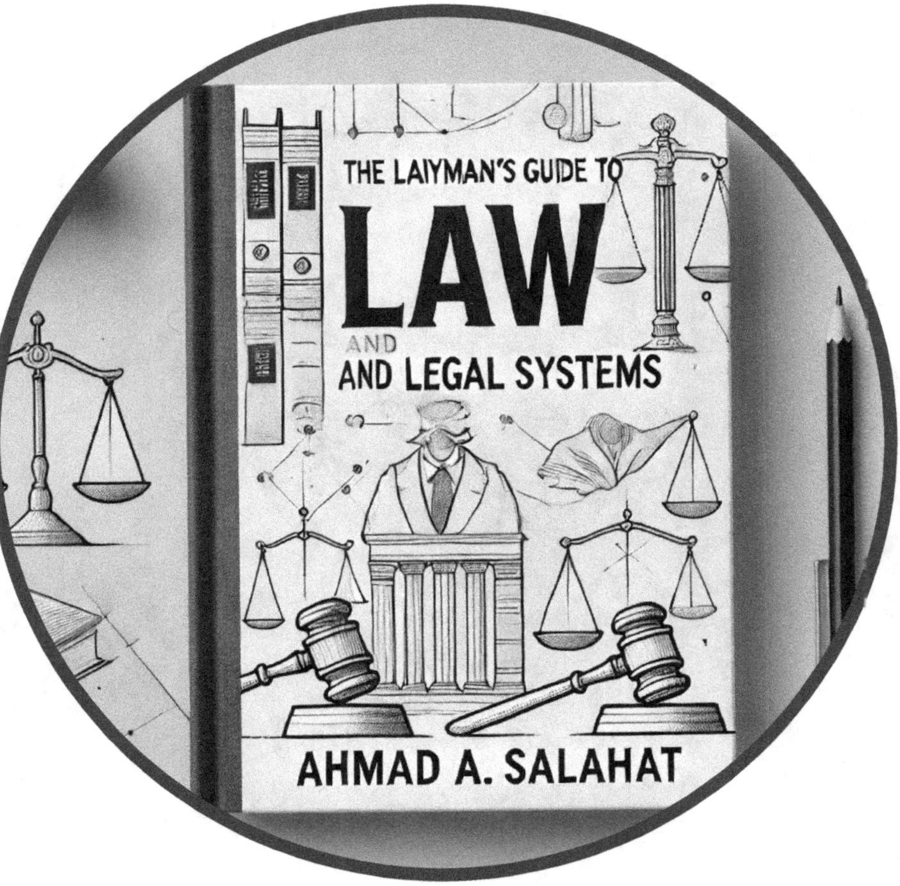

THE LAIYMAN'S GUIDE TO
LAW
AND LEGAL SYSTEMS

AHMAD A. SALAHAT

Ahmad A. Salahat

Counselor & Attorney at Law

Palestine

The Layman's Guide to Law and Legal Systems

By: Ahmad A. Salahat

Counselor and attorney
At Law

Contents

Warning 7
Hey there! 8
A heartfelt thank you to: 11
Chapter 1: The Basics: Understanding the Modern State 12
   Modern States: What Are They? 13
   Chapter 1: The Basics: Elements of the Modern State 15
   Governance of the modern state 16
   The law: 19
     Legal systems: 21
       Common Law: 21
   constitutional law 25
   Administrative law 26
   Criminal law 27
   taxation laws and public service 28
     Civil Law: 32
Chapter 2: Contracts and Contract Law 38
   Introduction to Contracts 38
     Essential Elements of a Contract 38
     Legality of Object: 39
     Types of Contracts 40
   Written Contracts 41
   Insurance Contracts **51**

Types of Insurance Contracts..56
Conclusion..61
Franchise Contracts: A Guide for Entrepreneurs...........................61
Final Thoughts for Entrepreneurs..68
Franchise Contracts vs. Building a Brand from Zero to Hero: A Comparison..68
Final Thoughts..75
Investment Contracts: Stocks, Trust Funds, and the CFD Trading Trap for Entrepreneurial Hopefuls...................................76
Comparing the Investment Types..80
Final Thoughts: Entrepreneurs Beware......................................81
Tech Bros and Startup Foundations: A Lawyer's Perspective.82
Final Thoughts: Legal First, Code Later......................................89

Chapter 3: Public Law and Its Reach into Everyday Life.....................91

  Criminal Law for the laymen:...91

Philosophy of Crime and Punishment..94
Types of Crimes and Why They Are Punished...........................95
The Intersection of Crime and Punishment................................97

  Criminal Procedure Law and Its Importance..................................98

  Constitutional Law and Administrative Law and Their Relationship with Criminal Justice:..102

  Taxation Law for The Laymen:...105

Chapter 4: Corporate Law—An Intersection of Civil Law and Public Law........110

Chapter 5: Understanding Legal Terminology.................................113

A	114
B	117
C	120
D	126
E	130
F	132
G	134
H	135
I	136
J	138
L	139
M	140
N	142
O	143
P	144
R	152
S	153
T	157
U	159
V	162
W	162
Where to Proceed Next	164
1. State-Specific Laws	164

2. Intellectual Property (IP) Law 164
3. International Law 165
- Treaties 165
- Customary International Law 165
- International Trade Law 165

When You Must Consult a Lawyer: Specific Cases and General Guidelines.....168

Copyright © 2024 by Ahmad A. Salahat 172

Warning

this book is intended for the layman/non legal professional to have foundational knowledge about the law, the state, legal systems and governance, meaning if u are a computer science major about to sign your first employment contract, you'll have a much better understanding of what each clause means, or if you're an entrepreneur and think you found your billion dollars idea, you'll have good insights about how to establish your corporate and have some legal compliance knowledge.

This is not legal advice because I'm not your lawyer and you did not pay me any attorney fees!

This book has no citations on purpose, don't take my word for anything, DO YOUR OWN RESEARCH!

Hey there!

So, you've picked up this book, huh? Well, let me tell you, you're in for a treat! But before we dive into the nitty-gritty of legal jargon and contract clauses, let's chat for a moment.

Have you ever found yourself staring at a contract, feeling like it's written in a whole different language? Or maybe you've had a legal question pop up, and you wished there was a simple, straightforward answer?

Well, my friend, you're not alone. The law can be a maze of confusion for the average person. But fear not! That's where this book comes in.

I'm not here to drown you in legalese or make your head spin with complicated theories. Nope, not at all. Instead, I want to take you on a journey through the world of law and legal systems, but in a way that's easy to understand, relatable, and dare I say it, maybe even a little fun? Then we can start progressing from conversational English to legal plain English!

If you've ever felt like the law is a mysterious beast lurking in the shadows, ready to pounce with its confusing contracts and complex legal jargon, then guess what? You're in the right place.

This book is for anyone who's ever stared blankly at a contract, scratched their head over a legal question, or simply wanted to feel more empowered when navigating the legal world. Whether you're a small business owner, a curious soul eager to demystify the law, or just someone who wants to level up their legal know-how, this book is your new best friend.

But hey, let's get real for a second. This isn't your typical dusty law textbook. Nope, not even close. This book is written in plain old' English – no fancy legalese here. So, if you're ready to embark on a journey through the wild and wonderful world of law, buckle up and let's dive in together!

As a counselor and attorney, I've seen firsthand how intimidating the legal world can be for folks who don't speak the language. That's why I've written this book – to be your guide, your translator, your friendly neighborhood legal guru.

Whether you're curious about contracts, wondering how the court system works, or just want to feel more confident in your legal know-how, I've got your back.

So, grab a comfy seat, maybe a cup of coffee (or tea, if that's your thing), and let's embark on this journey together. By the time you're done with this book, I promise you'll be looking at the law in a whole new light.

Ready? Let's do this!

Ahmad A. Salahat Counselor and Attorney at Law

A heartfelt thank you to:

Professor Anas M. Hassan, for imparting upon me the invaluable skills of thinking like a lawyer and nurturing my academic curiosity.

Attorney Mohammad Haddad, for being not just a mentor, but a guiding light throughout my journey in the legal world.

My dear parents, Ayesh and Rima, for their unwavering love, support, and encouragement, without which none of this would have been possible.

My siblings, Razan, Abd Al Hadi, and Rital, for their constant belief in me and for being my pillars of strength.

To all those who have inspired, encouraged, and stood by me along the way – thank you.

Yours, Ahmad A. Salahat Counselor and Attorney at Law

Chapter 1: The Basics: Understanding the Modern State

Alright, let's tackle the supposedly "boring stuff" – the theory of the modern state. But hey, trust me, it's not as dull as it sounds. We're going on a little journey back in time, about 6-7 thousand years back, to when our human civilizations were just starting to take shape. Picture it: states and kingdoms emerging, laying down the foundations that still influence us today.

First things first, what exactly is civilization? It's not just about fancy buildings and ancient artifacts (though those are pretty cool too, right?). Civilization is both the physical stuff – like cities, monuments, and all those breathtaking remnants of the past – and the intellectual legacy of a society. Think languages, culture, laws, and philosophies that shape how we live and think today. And guess what? We're still using ideas from those ancient civilizations, whether it's the Sumerians giving us writing or the Greeks introducing us to the wonders of democracy.

Now, for civilization to run smoothly, there needs to be some ground rules, right? That's where the law comes in. Imagine the state as an orchestra: you've got the legislative branch conducting the show, the judicial and executive branches as the musicians, and the law itself as the instruments being played. The audience? Well, that's society, reacting to the performance. And believe it or not, the core principles of legal rules haven't changed much since ancient times. Take Hammurabi's Code, with its famous "an eye for an eye" principle, or modern-day laws like the Jordanian Penal Code – they might look different on the surface, but strip away the details, and you'll find they're not so different after all.

So, what makes a modern state "modern," you ask? Well, that's where things get interesting – and that's exactly where this chapter kicks off!

Modern States: What Are They?

Ah, the age-old question: what exactly defines a modern state? Well, buckle up, because there's no one-size-fits-all answer here. It's kind of like asking different people what their favorite pizza topping is – you're bound to get a variety of answers depending on who you ask and where they stand politically.

For instance, toss this question to an anarchist, and they'll likely scoff and say something like, "States? Who needs 'em!" On the flip side, ask an alt-right enthusiast, and you might get an earful about the natural order of things and the role of authority.

Now, me? I'm more of a centrist kind of guy. I see validity in all these perspectives because let's face it, there's no definitive handbook on what makes a modern state tick. We can't exactly toss the concept into a test tube and analyze it under a microscope. But fear not! While we might not have all the answers, we can still piece together a pretty good picture by examining our current legal systems and political structures and comparing them to their historical counterparts.

One thing we can definitely point out is the shift towards individualism in many parts of the world. Gone are the days of strict patriarchy and divine rulers – now it's more about empowering the individual (at least in theory). But hey, don't get too hung up on the details. At the end of the day, modern states still operate under the notion of some higher authority, albeit with different rulebooks and ideologies depending on the era and the folks in charge.

So, here's the deal: I'm sharing my take on the matter, but I'm also nudging you to do a little digging of your own. Form your own opinions, do your own research – because hey, that's what being an informed citizen all is about.

Chapter 1: The Basics: Elements of the Modern State

Alright, let's break down the nuts and bolts of what makes up a modern state. There are four key elements in the mix, and they all play a crucial role:

a) The Population: First up, we've got the population – that's you, me, and everyone else living within the borders of the state. Think of us as the beating heart of the whole operation. Without people, well, there wouldn't be much of a state to speak of.

b) The Territory: Next, we've got the territory – the physical space that the state calls home. From bustling cities to sprawling countryside, every state needs its own chunk of land to function. It's where we live, work, and build all those fancy government buildings.

c) The Government: Now, here's where things get interesting – the government. This is the big boss, the top dog, the higher authority calling the shots over both the population and the territory. Whether it's elected officials, monarchs, or some other ruling body, the government is the glue that holds the whole shebang together.

d) Sovereignty: Last but not least, we have sovereignty. Now, this is a biggie. Sovereignty is basically the state's ultimate authority to govern itself without interference from external sources. It's like having your own little bubble of power and autonomy on the world stage.

So, why is all this important? Well, understanding these elements helps us grasp the inner workings of the modern state. And trust me, when it comes to navigating the legal landscape, a solid understanding of how the government operates is key.

Now, I know it might sound like a bit of a snooze fest, but stick with me. We're laying down the groundwork here, setting the stage for some juicier stuff down the line. So, grab a coffee, take a deep breath, and let's dive into the world of governance together.

Governance of the modern state

Ah, governance – now there's a topic that's anything but boring. It's the beating heart of the modern state, the engine that keeps the whole system running smoothly. So, what exactly is governance, you ask? Well, buckle up, because we're about to take a deep dive into the fascinating world of governing bodies and the art of running a state.

At its core, governance is all about decision-making and the exercise of authority. It's the process through which a government – whether it's a democratic regime, a monarchy, or something in between – manages the affairs of the state and ensures that things tick along like a well-oiled machine. Think of it as the ultimate balancing act, juggling the needs and interests of the population while keeping the ship steady in choppy waters.

But governance isn't just about calling the shots from on high. Oh no, it's much more nuanced than that. In a truly effective governance system, power is dispersed across various branches and levels of government, each with its own role to play. Take the classic example of the separation of powers – you've got the legislative branch making the laws, the executive branch enforcing them, and the judicial branch interpreting them. It's like a carefully choreographed dance, with each branch doing its part to ensure that no one gets too big for their britches.

Of course, governance isn't just about structure – it's also about values. A good governance system is rooted in principles like accountability, transparency, and fairness. It's about giving voice to the voiceless, protecting the rights of minorities, and ensuring that no one is above the law. In other words, it's about creating a society where everyone has a seat at the table and a stake in the game.

Now, I know what you're thinking – sounds great in theory, but how does it play out in practice? Well, that's where things get really interesting. Every government has its own unique set of challenges and opportunities, shaped by factors like history, culture, and geography. What works for one state might not work for another, and vice versa.

But here's the thing: while the specifics might vary, the underlying principles of good governance remain constant. Whether you're living under a parliamentary democracy in Europe or a federal republic in the Americas, the goal is always the same – to create a system that works for the people, by the people.

So, the next time you hear someone yammering on about governance, don't tune out – embrace it! Because understanding how our governments operate is the first step towards making them work better for everyone.

When we wrap our heads around how our governments operate, we unlock the power to actively participate in making them better. By tuning in to discussions about governance, we gain valuable insights that can lead to positive changes in our communities. We learn about different systems, structures, and decision-making processes, which empowers us to identify areas for improvement and hold our leaders accountable.

But it's not just about politics – governance extends its reach into various aspects of society, from corporate boardrooms to international organizations. By familiarizing ourselves with these different arenas, we become more informed citizens and active participants in shaping the world around us.

The law:

The Law is the glue that holds it all together, the maestro conducting the symphony of a functional state. But what exactly is this elusive concept that wields so much power and influence? Let's break it down.

At its core, the law is a set of rules and regulations that govern ***(remember governance from earlier?)*** human behavior within a society. It's the invisible hand guiding our actions, shaping our interactions, and ensuring order and justice prevail. Just like the conductor of an orchestra, the law orchestrates the harmonious functioning of the state, coordinating the various players and ensuring they stay in tune.

But the law is more than just a set of dos and don'ts – it's a reflection of our values, our ideals, and our collective vision for society and if engineering is applicable physics, the law is applicable philosophy. It embodies principles of fairness, equality, and justice, serving as a moral compass -that has been developing within societies since the dawn of civilization- to guide our actions.

Think of it this way: without the law, society would descend into chaos – it'd be like trying to play a symphony without a conductor. Sure, the individual musicians might be talented, but without someone to lead them, it'd be nothing but noise.

So, whether it's ensuring the rights of the individual, resolving disputes, or holding the powerful accountable, the law plays a vital role in shaping the fabric of our society. It's the bedrock upon which the modern state is built, the cornerstone of a functioning democracy.

But like any good conductor, the law isn't static – it's constantly evolving to meet the changing needs and values of society. From ancient codes of Hammurabi to modern-day statutes and precedents, the law adapts and grows alongside us, ensuring that justice is not just a lofty ideal, but a tangible reality for all.

So, the next time you find yourself pondering the intricacies of governance or the structure of the state, remember this: at the heart of it all lies the law, the maestro guiding the symphony of our collective existence.

Legal systems:

legal systems – now there's a topic that's as diverse as it is fascinating. When it comes to understanding how the law operates around the world, two systems stand out: common law and civil law (also known as the Latin or Roman-Germanic system). Let's dive into what makes each of these legal systems tick.

Common Law:

Originating in England and later spreading to countries like the United States, Canada, Australia, and India (thanks to British colonialism), common law is all about precedent. In this system, judges base their decisions on previous rulings and interpretations of the law, building up a body of case law over time. It's like a giant puzzle, with each court case adding another piece to the legal landscape.

Now, on the other side of the legal coin, we have civil law. This system traces its roots back to ancient Rome and is widely used in countries across Europe, Latin America, Africa, and parts of Asia. Unlike common law, which relies heavily on judicial precedent, civil law is codified – meaning the laws are written down in comprehensive legal codes. Think of it like following a recipe – everything you need to know is right there in black and white.

But wait, there's more! Civil law also places a strong emphasis on legal scholars and academic writings, with judges consulting legal doctrine and commentary to help interpret the law. It's like having a team of expert chefs offering advice on how to perfect your culinary creation.

So, what sets these two legal systems apart? Well, while both aim to achieve justice and maintain order within society, they take slightly different approaches to get there. Common law values flexibility and adaptability, allowing judges to interpret the law based on the specific facts of each case. Civil law, on the other hand, prioritizes clarity and predictability, with laws laid out in meticulous detail to leave little room for interpretation.

But despite their differences, common law and civil law share a common goal: to uphold the rule of law and ensure that justice is accessible to all. Whether you find yourself navigating the complexities of a common law jurisdiction or deciphering the intricacies of a civil law system, understanding the underlying principles of each legal system is key to navigating the ever-changing landscape of the law.

So, there you have it – a brief glimpse into the world of common law and civil law. Two distinct legal systems, each with its own rich history, traditions, and approaches to justice. And while they may differ in their methods, they both play a vital role in shaping the legal landscape of our world today.

First off, we have public law – the legal framework that governs the relationship between individuals and the state, as well as the structure and operation of government itself. Think of it as the rules of the game that keep the state running smoothly and ensure that the rights and responsibilities of both citizens and the government are clearly defined.

Within public law, there are several key sub-branches, including constitutional law, administrative law, and criminal law. Constitutional law deals with the fundamental principles and structures of government, such as the division of powers between different branches and levels of government and the protection of individual rights and freedoms. Administrative law, on the other hand, focuses on the actions and decisions of government agencies and officials, ensuring that they act within the bounds of their authority and in accordance with established procedures. And then there's criminal law, which governs offenses against the state and sets out the penalties for those who violate the law.

Now, let's turn our attention to civil law – the legal framework that governs disputes between individuals or organizations, often referred to as private law. Unlike public law, which deals with the relationship between individuals and the state, civil law deals with the relationships between individuals themselves. It's like the rulebook for everyday interactions, covering everything from contracts and property rights to torts and family law.

Within civil law, there are also various sub-branches, including contract law, property law, and tort law. Contract law governs agreements between parties, ensuring that promises are kept and obligations are fulfilled. Property law, on the other hand, deals with the ownership and use of land, buildings, and other assets. And then there's tort law, which addresses civil wrongs – such as negligence or defamation – and provides remedies for those who have been harmed by the actions of others.

So, there you have it – a brief overview of the branches of the law. Whether you find yourself grappling with the intricacies of public law or navigating the complexities of civil law, understanding the different branches and how they interact is key to navigating the legal landscape with confidence and now let us dive together in the different branches of both public and civil law.

constitutional law – the bedrock of any modern democratic society.

At its core, constitutional law is all about the fundamental principles and structures that govern a nation. It's like the rulebook that sets out the basic framework for how a country is run, laying down the ground rules for how power is distributed, how laws are made, and how rights are protected.

One of the key features of constitutional law is, you guessed it, the constitution itself – a written document (or set of documents) that serves as the supreme law of the land. This document outlines the structure of government, the powers and duties of different branches and levels of government, and the rights and freedoms of citizens.

But constitutional law isn't just about the words on paper – it's also about how those words are interpreted and applied in real life. That's where the judiciary comes in. Courts play a crucial role in interpreting the constitution and ensuring that the government acts within its bounds. Through a process known as judicial review, courts can strike down laws or government actions that are found to be unconstitutional, thereby upholding the rule of law and protecting individual rights.

Within the realm of constitutional law, there are also various subfields and areas of focus. These can include things like federalism – the division of powers between different levels of government – and separation of powers – the distribution of powers between different branches of government. There's also the protection of individual rights and freedoms, such as freedom of speech, religion, and association.

But perhaps most importantly, constitutional law is a living, breathing document – it evolves and adapts over time to reflect the changing needs and values of society. Through processes like constitutional amendment and judicial interpretation, the constitution remains relevant and responsive to the ever-changing dynamics of the modern world.

So, whether you're a legal scholar poring over the intricacies of constitutional doctrine or a concerned citizen advocating for your rights, understanding constitutional law is essential for navigating the complexities of our legal and political systems.

Administrative law – the often-overlooked yet incredibly important branch of legal studies that governs the actions and decisions of government agencies and officials.

At its core, administrative law is all about the rules and regulations that govern how government agencies operate and how they interact with the public. Think of it as the rulebook that keeps the wheels of government turning smoothly, ensuring that bureaucrats play by the rules and that the interests of citizens are protected.

One of the key principles of administrative law is the concept of administrative procedure – the rules and regulations that govern how government agencies make decisions, enforce regulations, and interact with the public. These procedures are designed to ensure transparency, fairness, and accountability in the way that government operates.

Administrative law also deals with issues of administrative discretion – the authority that government agencies have to make decisions within their areas of expertise. While administrative discretion is necessary for government to function effectively, it must be exercised within the bounds of the law and subject to oversight to prevent abuse.

Another important aspect of administrative law is the concept of judicial review – the power of the courts to review and overturn decisions made by government agencies that are found to be arbitrary, capricious, or contrary to law. This serves as a crucial check on the power of administrative agencies and helps to ensure that they operate within their delegated authority.

Within the realm of administrative law, there are also various specialized areas of focus, such as environmental law, immigration law, and healthcare law. These areas deal with specific issues and challenges faced by government agencies in their day-to-day operations and require a deep understanding of both the law and the underlying policy considerations.

So, whether you're a government official navigating the complexities of administrative procedure or a citizen seeking redress for a government action, understanding administrative law is essential for ensuring that government operates in a fair, transparent, and accountable manner.

Criminal law – the branch of legal studies that deals with offenses against the state and sets out the penalties for those who violate the law. It's like the sheriff of the legal world, keeping the peace and ensuring that justice is served.

At its core, criminal law is all about defining what constitutes a crime and prescribing the punishments for those who commit them. It's like a giant rulebook, outlining the dos and don'ts of society and laying down the consequences for breaking the rules.

One of the key principles of criminal law is the concept of culpability – the idea that individuals should only be punished for actions that they knowingly and willingly commit. This principle underpins the notion of mens rea, or the guilty mind, which requires prosecutors to prove that defendants had the intent to commit a crime.

Criminal law also deals with issues of procedure – the rules and regulations that govern how criminal cases are investigated, prosecuted, and adjudicated. These procedures are designed to ensure that defendants receive a fair trial and that their rights are protected throughout the criminal justice process.

Another important aspect of criminal law is the concept of punishment – the penalties that are imposed on individuals who are found guilty of committing crimes. These penalties can range from fines and probation to imprisonment and even death, depending on the severity of the offense and the laws of the jurisdiction.

Within the realm of criminal law, there are also various specialized areas of focus, such as drug offenses, white-collar crime, and violent crime. These areas require specialized knowledge and expertise to navigate, as they often involve complex legal and factual issues.

So, whether you're a prosecutor seeking justice for victims of crime or a defense attorney fighting to protect the rights of the accused, understanding criminal law is essential for ensuring that the wheels of justice keep turning and that society remains safe and secure.

taxation laws and public service – two crucial pillars of modern society that often go hand in hand. Let's unpack these important topics and explore how they intersect to shape the functioning of government and the provision of essential services to the public.

First off, taxation laws – the legal framework that governs how governments raise revenue to fund their operations and programs. Taxes are the lifeblood of any government, providing the resources needed to build infrastructure, maintain public services, and invest in the well-being of citizens.

Taxation laws come in many forms, from income taxes and sales taxes to property taxes and tariffs. Each type of tax serves a specific purpose and is governed by its own set of rules and regulations. For example, income taxes are levied on the earnings of individuals and businesses, while sales taxes are imposed on the purchase of goods and services.

But taxation isn't just about collecting money – it's also about promoting fairness and equity in society. Progressive tax systems, for instance, impose higher tax rates on those with higher incomes, ensuring that the burden of taxation is distributed fairly across society.

Now, let's talk about public service – the array of services and programs that governments provide to meet the needs of citizens and promote the common good. From education and healthcare to transportation and public safety, public services play a crucial role in enhancing the quality of life for everyone in society.

Public service is guided by principles of accountability, transparency, and efficiency, ensuring that taxpayer dollars are used wisely and effectively to deliver essential services to the public. This requires collaboration and cooperation among government agencies, as well as active engagement with citizens and stakeholders to identify needs and prioritize resources.

But taxation and public service are more than just abstract concepts – they have real-world implications for people's lives. Whether it's funding public schools, maintaining roads and bridges, or providing healthcare to those in need, taxation laws and public service are the cornerstones of a functioning society.

So, the next time you pay your taxes or interact with a public service, remember the important role that taxation laws and public service play in shaping the world around us. They may not always grab the headlines, but they're the backbone of our communities and the key to building a brighter future for all.

let's explore the specialized realm of public laws that govern various sectors and functions within society, ranging from military law to transportation regulations.

Firstly, military law, also known as military justice, comprises the set of laws and regulations that govern the conduct and behavior of members of the armed forces. Military law is essential for maintaining discipline, order, and accountability within military organizations. It covers a wide range of issues, including the rights and duties of service members, military offenses and punishments, and the procedures for military trials and courts-martial. Military law also intersects with international law, especially in areas such as the laws of armed conflict and the treatment of prisoners of war.

Next, security forces are governed by laws and regulations that define their roles, powers, and responsibilities in maintaining public safety and national security. These laws cover a broad spectrum of activities, including law enforcement, border security, counterterrorism, and intelligence gathering. Security forces must operate within the boundaries of the law, respecting the rights and freedoms of individuals while effectively addressing threats to public safety and national security.

Social services encompass a wide range of government programs and initiatives aimed at promoting the welfare and well-being of individuals and communities. Laws and regulations governing social services address issues such as healthcare, education, housing, employment, and social assistance. These laws are designed to ensure access to essential services, protect vulnerable populations, and address social inequalities. Social service providers must comply with legal requirements and standards to ensure the effective delivery of services and the protection of recipients' rights.

Transportation regulations govern the operation and management of various modes of transportation, including roadways, railways, airways, and waterways. These regulations cover areas such as vehicle safety standards, driver licensing and qualifications, traffic rules and regulations, and transportation infrastructure planning and development. Transportation laws aim to ensure the safety, efficiency, and accessibility of transportation systems while mitigating environmental impacts and promoting sustainable mobility.

In summary, specialized public laws play a crucial role in regulating specific sectors and functions within society, ensuring the orderly operation of essential services and the protection of public interests. These laws are tailored to address the unique challenges and complexities of each sector, balancing the need for effective governance with the rights and freedoms of individuals and communities.

Now, here's a little nugget of wisdom that applies regardless of which legal system you find yourself in: every public sector within your country or state operates under its own set of regulations. Whether it's a neatly codified statute in civil law systems or a tapestry of legal precedents and codified rules in common law jurisdictions, the law is intricately integrated into every aspect of governance.

So, here's my advice to you, dear reader: take a moment to pause and delve into your state's constitution. There, you'll find articles that describe the various government entities and their governing laws. Once you've got a handle on that, take another pause and dive into the specific statutes or laws that govern those entities. As you read, try to connect each article back to the relevant provisions in constitutional law.

The more laws you read, the clearer the picture becomes in your mind. You'll start to see how everything fits together, like pieces of a puzzle, forming a comprehensive understanding of how your government operates and how the law shapes its actions.

Civil Law:

Here's a general overview of the layout of civil law systems, presented in bullet points:

- **Codification:** Civil law systems are characterized by comprehensive legal codes that outline rights, obligations, and procedures in various areas of law.

- **Hierarchy of Laws:** Legal codes are organized hierarchically, with higher-ranking laws taking precedence over lower-ranking ones.

- **Division of Law:** Civil law codes typically cover multiple branches of law, including:

- Civil Law: Governs disputes between individuals or organizations, such as contracts, property rights, and torts.
- Commercial Law: Regulates business activities, including contracts, sales, and corporate governance.
- Family Law: Addresses matters such as marriage, divorce, child custody, and adoption.
- Corporate Law: addresses matters of corporate establishment, regulations and liabilities and it crosses paths with administrative law since corporates must be registered somehow within the state.

- **Articles and Sections:** Legal codes are divided into articles and sections, each addressing specific legal concepts or provisions.
- **Legal Principles:** Civil law systems often rely on legal principles such as clarity, predictability, and judicial independence to ensure fairness and consistency in the application of the law.
- **Judicial Interpretation:** While civil law codes provide a framework for legal decision-making, judges still play a role in interpreting and applying the law to individual cases.
- **Legal Commentary:** Legal scholars and commentators may provide additional analysis and interpretation of the law, helping to clarify its meaning and application.

This overview provides a snapshot of the structure and organization of civil law systems. In future prompts, we can delve deeper into each of these aspects, exploring their significance and implications within the broader legal framework.

Now, let's delve into civil law, the cornerstone of people's everyday lives. Within civil law, there exists the concept of civil obligations, which essentially curtail an individual's absolute freedom by binding them to specific actions or refraining from others. These obligations stem from five globally recognized sources:

1- **Contract:** Contracts represent the most prevalent source of obligations. A contract is essentially a binding agreement between two or more parties to either perform or abstain from a particular action. Contrary to a common misconception, contracts aren't solely confined to paperwork; they can also be oral agreements. For instance, when X hails a taxi, directs it to a destination, pays the fare upon arrival, a contract has been fulfilled. Both parties have agreed to a transaction where compensation and legal validity exist.

2- **Singular Will:** In this scenario, the consent of one party alone is sufficient to establish an obligation. For example, if a restaurant advertises that anyone ordering a certain meal will receive a complimentary soda, failing to provide the soda to customers who ordered the specified meal would constitute a breach of legal obligation.

3- **Torts:** Torts refer to wrongful acts that give rise to civil obligations. For instance, if someone runs a red light and collides with another person's car, the individual who disregarded the traffic signal would be liable for the resulting damages. This includes compensating the affected parties for any physical, emotional, or material harm caused.

4- **The Law:** At times, legal obligations are established directly by the law itself. For example, under Palestinian labor law, an employer is mandated to provide compensation to employees upon resignation. This compensation, typically equating to a month's salary for each year of service, is not subject to negotiation or agreement between the parties; it is a legal requirement imposed by statute.

5- **Positive and/or Negative Actions:** This refers to situations where individuals take affirmative or corrective actions that result in civil obligations. For instance, if a neighbor is abroad and their fence collapses due to severe winter winds, leaving their yard vulnerable to intrusion, and you take it upon yourself to rebuild the fence to prevent further damage, the owner now owes you reimbursement for the repairs undertaken. This obligation arises from the positive action you took to mitigate potential harm.

In summary, all the aforementioned sources of obligations derive their authority and enforceability from the law itself. Whether stemming from contracts, singular will, torts, or statutory requirements, these obligations are grounded in legal principles and are binding upon the parties involved.

Furthermore, certain statutes and case precedents establish limitations on what individuals can agree upon, define the scope of tortious conduct, and outline default clauses to govern situations where parties fail to reach a mutual agreement. These legal provisions serve to ensure fairness, uphold public policy objectives, and provide clarity and consistency in the resolution of disputes. They act as guardrails within the legal framework, guiding parties toward equitable outcomes and reinforcing the rule of law in society.

Ultimately, the law serves as a cornerstone of society, harmonizing justice and stability with societal values and aspirations. Its overarching goal is to enhance the quality of life for every citizen, fostering a stable economy and providing a fertile environment for innovation to thrive. By upholding the rule of law, we ensure fairness, promote social cohesion, and pave the way for progress and prosperity for generations to come.

This interconnectedness is evident in legal articles within statutes, which often refrain from specifying individuals and instead address abstract ideas or situations. For instance, consider the provision stating, "whoever turns 18 years of age is considered a consenting adult." This aligns seamlessly with another civil law article stipulating that "the Gregorian calendar is used to calculate legal limitations or age." In turn, this requirement lines up with yet another article mandating that "for a contract to be valid, both parties must have legal true consent." Through this alignment, the law becomes integrated and self-explanatory, aiming to achieve the maximum amount of justice possible by ensuring consistency and coherence across legal provisions.

(The reader is encouraged to read related civil laws enforceable in their state.)

Chapter 2: Contracts and Contract Law.

Introduction to Contracts

Contracts form the backbone of our day-to-day transactions and are a fundamental component of civil law. Whether it's purchasing a coffee, signing up for a phone plan, or securing a multi-million-dollar business deal, contracts govern the agreements we enter into, providing a framework for the obligations and rights of the parties involved.

A contract, in its simplest form, is a binding agreement between two or more parties to do or not do something. This agreement can be oral, written, or implied by conduct, but to be enforceable by law, certain elements must be present. These elements are what distinguish a mere understanding from a legally binding contract.

Essential Elements of a Contract

Offer and Acceptance:

A contract starts with an offer from one party and the acceptance of that offer by another. The offer must be clear, definite, and communicated to the other party. Acceptance must match the terms of the offer without any changes—otherwise, it becomes a counteroffer, which the original offeror must then accept.

To illustrate, consider billboard advertisements. Imagine you're on your way to work and see a billboard stating, "Buy 2 packs of cigarettes, get 1 free." Legally, this is considered an offer. When you go to the supermarket and ask for the two packs of cigarettes, you are accepting the offer, thus forming a legally binding contract.

The same principle applies to hailing a taxi. Waving at a cab is seen as an invitation to contract (in this case, a transportation contract). When you tell the driver your destination, that's the offer, and the driver starting to move towards your destination is the acceptance. The fare, typically calculated by a meter, is agreed upon through conduct.

Consideration:

Consideration is what each party agrees to give or do for the other. It can be money, goods, services, or even a promise to refrain from doing something. The key is that both parties must provide something of value for the contract to be enforceable. In some legal systems, the law may impose certain conditions or limitations on what can constitute valid consideration.

Intention to Create Legal Relations:

Not all agreements are meant to be legally binding. For a contract to be enforceable, the parties involved must intend to create a legal obligation. This intention is generally presumed in commercial agreements but not in social or domestic arrangements.

For example, if someone tries to buy an illegal substance and then decides to sue the dealer because they were unhappy with the product's quality, they wouldn't have a valid case. The law does not recognize or enforce agreements related to illegal activities, highlighting the importance of lawful intent when entering into contracts.

Capacity to Contract:

The parties involved must have the legal capacity to enter into a contract. Generally, this means they must be of legal age and sound mind. In some jurisdictions, certain individuals, such as minors or those with mental incapacities, may have limited capacity to contract, and agreements involving such individuals might be void or voidable.

Legality of Object:

The purpose of the contract must be legal. Contracts that involve illegal activities or go against public policy are void and unenforceable. For instance, an agreement to commit a crime or to defraud someone cannot form the basis of a legally binding contract.

Types of Contracts

Contracts can take many forms, depending on the nature of the agreement and the parties involved. Some common types include:

1. **Bilateral Contracts**
    - Most contracts are bilateral, where both parties make promises to each other. For example, in a sales contract, one party promises to deliver goods, while the other promises to pay for them.

2. **Unilateral Contracts**
    - In a unilateral contract, one party makes a promise in exchange for the other party performing a specific act. A common example is a reward contract, where one party promises to pay if the other finds and returns a lost item.

3. **Express Contracts**
    - These are contracts where the terms are explicitly stated, either orally or in writing. Both parties know exactly what they are agreeing to, leaving little room for interpretation.

4. **Implied Contracts**
    - Implied contracts are formed by the behavior or circumstances of the parties, rather than written or spoken words. For instance, when you visit a doctor, it is implied

that you will pay for the services provided, even though you may not have explicitly discussed it.

Performance and Breach of Contracts

Performance refers to the completion of the contractual obligations as agreed upon by the parties involved. Once all parties fulfill their respective duties, the contract is considered discharged or completed. However, when a party fails to perform as promised, it results in a breach of contract.

Breaches can range from minor to material, depending on the extent of the failure to meet the agreed-upon terms. Remedies for a breach of contract might include damages, where the breaching party pays monetary compensation; specific performance, where a court orders the breaching party to fulfill their obligations; or cancellation and restitution, which involves terminating the contract and returning any benefits exchanged.

This connects back to the sources of obligations previously discussed, as breaches of contract directly impact the enforceability and fulfillment of those obligations.

Written Contracts

Written contracts are formal agreements that are documented in writing and signed by the parties involved. These contracts are common in various aspects of daily life, such as employment contracts, leases, and phone service agreements. Let's break down some common clauses found in these contracts and explain what they mean in layman's terms, with a narrow overview of the main elements of each contract.

1. Employment Contracts: Employment contracts outline the terms of the relationship between an employer and an employee. Here are a few common clauses:

- **Job Description:** This clause specifies the duties and responsibilities of the employee. It ensures that both parties understand the role the employee will play within the organization.

- **Salary and Benefits:** This clause details the compensation the employee will receive, including salary, bonuses, health insurance, and other benefits. It may also include information on how and when the employee will be paid.

- **Confidentiality:** Often, employment contracts contain a confidentiality clause, which requires the employee to keep certain information about the company private, both during and after their employment.

- **Termination:** This clause outlines the conditions under which either party can terminate the employment relationship. It may include notice periods, reasons for termination, and any severance pay the employee is entitled to.

2. lease contracts: A lease contract, often referred to as a rental agreement, is a legally binding document that outlines the terms under which one party (the lessee or tenant) agrees to rent property owned by another party (the lessor or landlord). Unlike a purchase agreement where ownership is transferred, a lease involves temporary possession and usage of property in exchange for regular payments, typically rent. This kind of contract is common for renting apartments, houses, or commercial spaces, and its clauses are designed to protect both parties by clarifying their rights and obligations.

Let's dive into some of the typical clauses found in lease contracts and how they function in everyday life:

1. Rent Payment Clause

This clause defines the amount of rent, the due date for payment (e.g., the 1st of every month), and any penalties for late payment. In a lease, failure to pay rent on time is considered a breach of contract, potentially leading to eviction or penalties. Often, there's also a grace period (e.g., 3-5 days after the due date) before late fees apply.

In simple terms, this part of the lease is all about how much you owe, when you need to pay it, and what happens if you miss the deadline.

2. Security Deposit Clause

This clause outlines how much the tenant must pay as a security deposit, which is held by the landlord to cover any potential damages or unpaid rent. At the end of the lease, if no damages have occurred and rent is fully paid, this deposit is usually refunded.

Think of the security deposit as a financial safety net for the landlord in case the property isn't returned in good condition.

3. Duration (Term) of Lease

The duration clause specifies the length of the lease—typically six months, one year, or longer. Some leases automatically renew unless notice is given, while others end on a specific date.

This clause makes sure both parties know how long the lease lasts and what happens once that period ends. It's crucial for planning whether you're staying long-term or looking for a new place.

4. Maintenance and Repairs

Here, the lease specifies the responsibilities of both the tenant and the landlord regarding maintenance and repairs. Generally, landlords are responsible for major repairs (plumbing, electrical issues), while tenants are required to keep the property in good condition and report any damages promptly.

In layman's terms, if the water heater breaks, it's probably the landlord's job to fix it, but if you break a window, you'll likely be responsible for the repair.

5. Use of Premises

This clause sets the conditions under which the leased property can be used. For example, it might limit the number of people living in the apartment or restrict running a business from a residential rental.

It's essentially a way of saying, "This property is for living, not for turning it into a commercial bakery or subletting to your 12 friends."

6. Termination Clause

This clause explains how and under what conditions the lease can be terminated before its official end date. It could be due to mutual agreement, violation of lease terms, or for non-payment of rent. Some leases include an early termination fee if the tenant leaves before the lease expires.

In everyday terms, this section answers the question, "How can I get out of this lease early?"—but usually at a cost.

7. Renewal Clause

The renewal clause lays out what happens at the end of the lease term. Does the contract renew automatically, or do the parties need to sign a new lease? Some leases transition into a month-to-month agreement unless action is taken by the tenant or landlord.

This part essentially tells you what happens after your lease is up: will you need to renegotiate, or will things keep rolling along as they were?

8. Subletting and Assigning

Subletting occurs when the tenant rents out the property to a third party. Some leases explicitly prohibit subletting, while others may allow it with the landlord's written permission. Assigning the lease means transferring it entirely to another person, which may also be restricted.

In simple terms, if you're leaving town for six months and want to rent the place out to someone else, you need to check this clause to see if that's allowed.

How Lease Contracts Differ from Other Similar Contracts

- **Lease vs. Rental Agreement:** A lease typically involves a longer-term commitment (e.g., one year), whereas a rental agreement is often month-to-month. A rental agreement can be changed more frequently (such as rent price or terms), while a lease locks both parties into the terms for the agreed duration.

- **Lease vs. License Agreement:** A lease gives the tenant a legal interest in the property for the duration of the lease, meaning the tenant has exclusive possession. A license, on the other hand, grants only permission to use the property but not exclusive possession. For example, a hotel room is under a license agreement, not a lease.

- **Lease vs. Employment Contract:** While both lease and employment contracts bind parties to agreed terms, an employment contract governs the relationship between employer and employee, detailing job responsibilities, wages, and working conditions. A lease, by contrast, is concerned with property usage and rental payments.

- **Lease vs. Service Contract:** A service contract (like a phone contract) is an agreement where one party provides services to another for a fee. It's typically more flexible and less focused on the physical possession of property, as opposed to a lease that involves occupying a physical space.

3. Phone Service Agreements: A phone service contract, also known as a mobile service agreement, is a legally binding agreement between a service provider (e.g., a mobile carrier) and the customer, outlining the terms under which phone services are provided in exchange for regular payments. These contracts often involve a fixed-term commitment (e.g., 12, 24 months), and they define what services will be delivered, the costs, and the obligations of both parties. Let's break down some common clauses you'll encounter in a phone service contract and what they mean in simple, practical terms:

1. Service Plan

This clause outlines the type of phone plan you've chosen, including data limits, call minutes, text messaging, and any additional features like roaming or international calling. The service plan also specifies the monthly charges based on the selected package.

In layman's terms, this section is all about how much data, talk time, and texts you get every month, and what it's going to cost you.

2. Term Length

The term length is the duration of the contract, typically ranging from 12 to 24 months. During this period, both parties are expected to fulfill the agreed terms, with the customer making monthly payments and the carrier providing uninterrupted service.

This part essentially locks you in for a set period—say, two years—during which you're committed to the provider, and breaking the contract early could come with penalties.

3. Early Termination Clause

This clause explains the conditions under which either party can terminate the contract before the end of the agreed term. Early termination usually results in fees, which are designed to recoup the cost of subsidized phones or services already provided by the carrier.

In everyday terms, if you decide to leave your phone provider before your contract is up, you'll likely have to pay a fee to break free.

4. Data Usage Limits

Most phone contracts come with a specified data allowance, after which you might experience reduced speeds, additional charges, or restricted access to certain services. This clause details how much data you can use each month and the consequences of exceeding that limit.

In simple terms, if you're binge-watching videos and hit your data cap, your internet might slow down or you could get hit with extra charges.

5. Roaming and International Usage

This clause outlines the charges and limitations associated with using your phone outside your home country or service area. Some contracts include free roaming within certain regions, while others may charge extra for calls, texts, or data used abroad.

So, if you're planning a vacation, this section tells you whether or not you'll need to pay extra for making calls or using the internet while overseas.

6. Device Subsidy and Payment Plan

Some phone contracts include a subsidy for the cost of the phone itself, allowing you to spread payments over the life of the contract (e.g., 24 monthly payments for a new smartphone). This clause specifies whether the phone is included in your monthly bill and what happens if you leave the contract early.

In everyday terms, this is how you can get a new phone without paying for it all at once. However, if you break the contract early, you'll likely need to pay off the rest of the phone in a lump sum.

7. Service Availability and Coverage

This clause defines the extent of the network's coverage and any limitations that may arise based on your location. It also outlines the provider's responsibility for maintaining service but often includes a disclaimer that coverage may not be available in all areas.

In simple language, it's the section that says, "We'll do our best to keep you connected, but we can't promise perfect service in rural or remote areas."

8. Billing and Payment

This clause covers how and when you're billed, the available payment methods, and any penalties for late payments. It also outlines your responsibilities as a customer to review and pay your bills on time.

It's basically the nitty-gritty of how much you owe each month, how you can pay, and what happens if you miss a payment (spoiler: late fees).

9. Fair Usage Policy

Many phone service contracts include a fair usage policy, which places limits on how you can use unlimited data, texts, or calls. It's designed to prevent customers from abusing the system by excessively using the network's resources.

In layman's terms, if you're using way more data than the average user—like setting up a mobile hotspot for your entire apartment complex—your provider might slow your speeds or charge you extra.

10. Dispute Resolution

This clause outlines how disputes between the customer and the service provider will be handled, often requiring arbitration or mediation rather than litigation. It may also explain the steps customers can take to raise concerns about billing or service issues.

This section is your go-to if things go south, providing a roadmap for resolving any disagreements over service or billing without having to go to court.

How Phone Service Contracts Differ from Other Similar Contracts

- **Phone Service Contracts vs. Employment Contracts:** Employment contracts involve job duties, compensation, and working conditions, whereas a phone service contract is about providing a telecommunications service. The former governs a working relationship, while the latter focuses on access to phone and internet services.

- **Phone Service Contracts vs. Lease Contracts:** A lease contract gives you possession of property, whereas a phone service contract gives you access to a service (calls, texts, data). Both may involve fixed-term commitments, but the core difference is that leases deal with physical spaces, while phone contracts provide network access.

- **Phone Service Contracts vs. Service Agreements:** Like a phone service contract, general service agreements (e.g., for internet or utilities) involve payment for a service. However, phone contracts often include specific clauses related to device subsidies, network usage, and data limits, which aren't typically found in other service agreements.

Phone service contracts are an essential part of modern life, offering clarity on what services will be provided, at what cost, and under what conditions. Whether you're signing up for a new plan or renewing an existing one, it's important to understand the key terms of the agreement to avoid unexpected fees or limitations down the road.

Reading the fine print and asking questions can save you from surprises—whether it's hidden fees for going over your data limit or penalties for leaving your provider early. By understanding the key clauses, you'll be able to make informed decisions and choose the service plan that works best for your needs.

Insurance Contracts

An insurance contract is a legally binding agreement between an insurer (the company providing the insurance) and the insured (the individual or entity purchasing the insurance), where the insurer agrees to compensate the insured for certain losses or damages in exchange for regular premium payments. Insurance contracts can cover various types of risks, including health, life, auto, property, and liability. Let's break down some common clauses in insurance contracts and explain what they mean in practical, layman's terms:

1. Premium

This clause outlines the amount the insured must pay to maintain the insurance policy, either as a one-time payment or on a recurring basis (e.g., monthly, quarterly, or annually). The premium is determined by factors such as the type of coverage, the insured's risk profile, and the value of what is being insured.

In simple terms, this is the price tag for your insurance—the amount you pay regularly to stay covered.

2. Coverage

The coverage clause defines what the insurance policy protects against, including specific risks, damages, or losses that the insurer agrees to compensate for. It also specifies the maximum amount the insurer will pay out in the event of a claim.

In everyday language, this part tells you what's covered—whether it's your health, car, home, or something else—and how much money you'll get if something goes wrong.

3. Exclusions

This clause details what is *not* covered by the insurance policy. Common exclusions might include pre-existing conditions in health insurance, acts of war or terrorism in life insurance, or intentional damage in property insurance.

In simple terms, these are the things your insurance won't pay for, like if you wreck your car on purpose or try to claim damage from a flood in an area that's not covered.

4. Deductible

The deductible is the amount the insured must pay out of pocket before the insurer begins to cover the rest of the claim. This amount is predetermined and can vary depending on the policy and the type of insurance.

In everyday terms, think of the deductible as the portion of the cost you have to handle before your insurance kicks in. For example, if your car insurance deductible is $500 and your repair costs $2,000, you'll pay the first $500, and the insurance covers the rest.

5. Policy Limit

The policy limit defines the maximum amount the insurer will pay out on a claim or over the life of the insurance policy. Some policies may have separate limits for different types of claims (e.g., bodily injury vs. property damage in auto insurance).

In simple terms, this is the cap on how much the insurance company will pay you. If your policy limit is $100,000 and the total damage is $150,000, you'll only get $100,000 from the insurer.

6. Claim Procedure

This clause explains the steps you need to follow to file a claim and receive compensation for a loss. It usually requires the insured to notify the insurer within a certain time frame and provide documentation of the loss or damage.

In simple terms, this section tells you what you need to do if you want to get paid after something bad happens, like calling the insurance company and sending them proof of the damage.

7. Indemnity

Indemnity refers to the insurer's obligation to compensate the insured for a covered loss. The aim of this clause is to restore the insured to their financial position before the loss occurred, without allowing them to profit from the insurance claim.

In layman's terms, this means the insurance is there to make things right again after a loss, but you can't use it to make a profit. For example, if your car is totaled, the insurer will pay you the value of the car before the accident, not more than that.

8. Subrogation

This clause allows the insurer to step into the shoes of the insured and seek compensation from a third party that caused the loss. For example, if your insurance pays for damages caused by a negligent driver, the insurer may then sue that driver to recover the money they paid you.

In simple terms, after the insurance company compensates you, they can go after the person who caused the damage to get their money back.

9. Grace Period

The grace period is the amount of time the insured has to pay the premium after it's due before the policy is canceled. If payment is not made within this period, the insurer may terminate the contract.

In practical terms, this gives you a little wiggle room if you miss a payment. So, if your payment is due on the 1st and you're a bit late, you might have until the 15th to pay before your coverage is canceled.

10. Cancellation Clause

This clause outlines the conditions under which the insurance policy can be canceled by either the insurer or the insured. It often includes a requirement for notice, stating how many days in advance one party must inform the other before canceling the policy.

In simple terms, this section says how and when you or the insurance company can end the contract—like if you stop paying premiums or the insurer decides they no longer want to insure you after a certain risk emerges.

Types of Insurance Contracts

Insurance contracts come in many forms, each designed to protect against different types of risks. The most common types include health/medical insurance, vehicle insurance, and personal injury insurance, such as car accident coverage. Each type of insurance serves a specific purpose, offering peace of mind and financial protection in various areas of life. Let's explore these in more detail and look at what makes each type unique:

1. Health/Medical Insurance

Health insurance is designed to cover medical expenses incurred by the insured, such as doctor visits, hospital stays, surgeries, and prescription medications. Depending on the policy, it may also cover preventive care like vaccines and screenings. Health insurance contracts typically specify what treatments and services are covered, as well as any co-pays, deductibles, and limits on coverage.

- **Coverage:** Health insurance can range from basic plans that only cover essential services to comprehensive plans that include mental health, dental, and vision care.
- **Premiums and Deductibles:** These policies usually involve regular premium payments and out-of-pocket costs like deductibles (the amount you pay before insurance kicks in) and co-pays (a small fee for each service).
- **Exclusions:** Most health insurance policies have exclusions for certain treatments, such as cosmetic surgery, experimental therapies, or alternative treatments not recognized by the medical community.

In everyday terms, health insurance is there to help you pay for your healthcare needs—whether it's a routine check-up or an unexpected emergency—while limiting the financial burden on you.

2. Vehicle Insurance

Vehicle insurance, often referred to as auto insurance, provides financial protection against damages to your vehicle and liabilities that may arise from accidents involving your vehicle. Vehicle insurance is mandatory in most countries, with policies covering a range of situations such as collisions, theft, and vandalism.

- **Liability Coverage:** This is the most basic form of vehicle insurance and is often legally required. It covers damages

or injuries that you cause to others in an accident, such as medical bills or property damage.
- **Collision Coverage:** This part of the policy covers damages to your own vehicle resulting from a collision, regardless of who is at fault.
- **Comprehensive Coverage:** This covers damages to your vehicle that are not caused by a collision, such as theft, fire, or natural disasters.
- **Personal Injury Protection (PIP):** This is included in some policies and covers medical expenses for injuries sustained in an accident, regardless of fault.
- **Uninsured/Underinsured Motorist Coverage:** Protects you if you are in an accident caused by someone who does not have sufficient insurance to cover your damages.

In simple terms, vehicle insurance is there to protect you from financial loss if you're involved in a car accident or if your vehicle is damaged or stolen. Whether you're at fault or not, this type of insurance ensures you're not left footing the bill alone.

---

3. Car Accident Injury Insurance

This type of insurance is specifically geared toward covering medical costs, rehabilitation, and even lost wages if you're injured in a car accident. It can be part of your vehicle insurance (like personal injury protection) or a separate policy.

- **Medical Payments Coverage (Med Pay):** Covers medical expenses for you and your passengers after an accident, regardless of fault.
- **Bodily Injury Liability:** Covers medical expenses for other drivers and passengers if you are at fault in an accident.
- **PIP (Personal Injury Protection):** As mentioned earlier, PIP goes beyond medical payments to cover lost wages and other expenses like child care if you're unable to work due to injuries.

This type of coverage is especially important in situations where injuries are serious and lead to long-term medical treatment or disability. Essentially, it ensures you get the medical help you need without depleting your savings or income in the process.

---

4. Life Insurance

Life insurance provides a financial safety net for your family or beneficiaries in the event of your death. There are two main types: term life insurance and whole life insurance.

- **Term Life Insurance:** Provides coverage for a set period, like 10, 20, or 30 years. If you pass away during the term, the policy pays a death benefit to your beneficiaries.
- **Whole Life Insurance:** This provides lifelong coverage and includes a savings component, where the insured can accumulate cash value over time.

Life insurance gives your loved one's financial security, covering expenses like funeral costs, outstanding debts, and providing income replacement.

5. Homeowner's Insurance

Homeowner's insurance protects your home and its contents from risks such as fire, theft, or natural disasters. It typically covers both the structure of the home and personal belongings, and also includes liability coverage in case someone is injured on your property.

- **Structure Coverage:** Covers the cost to repair or rebuild your home if it's damaged by a covered event (like fire or storms).
- **Personal Property Coverage:** This covers items inside your home, like furniture, electronics, and appliances, if they are stolen or damaged.
- **Liability Coverage:** Protects you if someone is injured on your property and decides to sue you.

In short, homeowner's insurance ensures that if something happens to your home, you're not left paying for all the damages out of pocket.

6. Travel Insurance

Travel insurance covers unexpected costs that may arise during a trip, such as medical emergencies, trip cancellations, lost luggage, or flight delays.

- **Trip Cancellation Coverage:** Reimburses you if you need to cancel your trip due to covered reasons like illness or severe weather.
- **Medical Coverage:** Provides coverage for medical emergencies that occur while traveling, especially important for international travel.
- **Baggage and Personal Effects Coverage:** Protects against the loss or theft of your belongings during your trip.

Travel insurance is all about safeguarding your trip, ensuring that you're protected against unforeseen events that could disrupt your plans or cost you money.

Conclusion

Each type of insurance contract offers specific protections against risks, whether it's your health, vehicle, home, or travels. Understanding these contracts and their common clauses can help you make informed decisions about your coverage, ensuring you're protected when unexpected events arise. Insurance contracts are designed to minimize financial hardship, giving you peace of mind knowing that you're covered in different aspects of life. Whether it's health coverage, auto insurance, or life insurance, these contracts form an essential part of financial planning and risk management.

Franchise Contracts: A Guide for Entrepreneurs

A franchise contract is an agreement between a franchiser (the business that owns the brand and business model) and a franchisee (the entrepreneur who wants to open and operate the franchise). This type of contract is a powerful tool for entrepreneurs looking to invest in an established brand and reduce the risk associated with starting a new business from scratch. However, franchise contracts come with obligations and commitments that must be carefully understood before entering into the agreement. Here's a breakdown of franchise contracts, focusing on key terms and clauses aimed at helping entrepreneurs navigate the process.

What is a Franchise Contract?

A franchise contract is a legally binding agreement that allows the franchisee to use the franchiser's brand, trademarks, products, and business model in exchange for various payments, such as royalties and franchise fees. It outlines the rights and responsibilities of both parties and serves as a road map for operating the franchise successfully.

In simple terms, a franchise contract gives entrepreneurs the right to run their own business while benefiting from an established brand and support system. However, it also binds the franchisee to certain rules and standards set by the franchiser.

Key Clauses in Franchise Contracts

1. **Franchise Fees and Royalties**
    - **Franchise Fees:** This is the upfront cost you pay to gain the rights to operate the franchise. It's usually a one-time payment and can range widely depending on the brand.
    - **Royalties:** These are ongoing payments (usually a percentage of your revenue) that you make to the franchiser for the continued use of their brand and systems.

    Entrepreneur's Tip: Understand what you're paying for—many franchisers provide initial training, marketing support, and continuous updates to their business model in exchange for these fees.

2. **Territorial Rights**
    - This clause outlines the geographic area where the franchisee is allowed to operate. It may grant exclusive rights within a certain area, preventing the franchiser from opening another franchise nearby.

Entrepreneur's Tip: Make sure the territory is large enough to provide growth potential and that you understand whether your rights are exclusive or shared with other franchisees.

3. **Operational Standards**
   - Franchise contracts often come with strict guidelines about how the business should be run. This includes product offerings, customer service, and marketing strategies. These rules help maintain brand consistency across all franchises.

Entrepreneur's Tip: While you may have some flexibility, be prepared to follow detailed instructions on day-to-day operations. Deviation from these guidelines could result in penalties or even termination of the contract.

4. **Training and Support**
   - The franchiser typically offers initial training on how to operate the franchise, as well as ongoing support. This could cover everything from hiring employees to managing inventory and marketing.

Entrepreneur's Tip: Make sure to evaluate the quality and scope of the training. Good support can be a critical factor in your success as a franchisee.

5. **Marketing Fees**

- Many franchisers require franchisees to contribute to a national or regional advertising fund. This fee supports brand-wide marketing efforts, which help attract customers.

Entrepreneur's Tip: Ask how the marketing fees are used and whether you have a say in local advertising efforts. Some contracts allow flexibility for additional local promotions.

6. **Duration and Renewal**
    - Franchise contracts typically last for a set period, such as 5 to 20 years. The contract will outline the terms for renewing the agreement at the end of this period.

Entrepreneur's Tip: Understand what's required for renewal—some franchisors may require additional fees or updated agreements, while others may allow a smooth extension of your contract.

7. **Non-Compete Clause**
    - This clause restricts the franchisee from opening a competing business, either during or after the term of the franchise agreement. It ensures that franchisees don't use the franchiser's knowledge and customer base to start a rival business.

Entrepreneur's Tip: Make sure the non-compete clause is reasonable and doesn't overly limit your future business opportunities after the franchise contract ends.

8. **Termination Conditions**
    - The contract will specify conditions under which the agreement can be terminated, either by the franchisee or the franchiser. This could include failure to meet sales targets, breach of operational guidelines, or failure to pay fees.

Entrepreneur's Tip: Understand both your rights and the franchiser's rights to terminate the contract. Some contracts allow the franchiser to terminate with little notice, so ensure you're protected.

9. **Dispute Resolution**
    - This clause outlines how disagreements between the franchiser and franchisee will be handled, such as through mediation, arbitration, or legal proceedings.

Entrepreneur's Tip: Review the dispute resolution process carefully. Arbitration is often faster and less costly than litigation, but it may limit your ability to appeal a decision.

Types of Franchise Models

As an entrepreneur, it's important to know that there are different franchise models. Each comes with its own opportunities and risks:

1. **Product Distribution Franchise:** The franchisee is granted the right to distribute the franchiser's products, but typically with less control over the overall business model (e.g., car dealerships).
2. **Business Format Franchise:** The franchisee adopts the entire business model of the franchiser, including operational procedures, marketing, and services (e.g., fast food chains).
3. **Investment Franchise:** This model is often for larger-scale franchises where the franchisee makes a significant financial investment but hires others to manage day-to-day operations (e.g., hotels).
4. **Job Franchise:** Usually for smaller-scale, home-based operations where the franchisee performs the work themselves (e.g., cleaning services, lawn care).

Why Franchise Contracts Matter for Entrepreneurs

Franchise contracts provide entrepreneurs with a unique opportunity to leverage an existing brand's reputation, customer base, and proven business model. This reduces much of the risk associated with starting a business from scratch. However, the contract also sets boundaries and expectations for how you operate, and these must be followed closely.

- **Pros:** You get a turnkey business with support and a built-in customer base. This can be especially appealing for first-time business owners.
- **Cons:** You're bound by the terms of the contract, which may limit your ability to innovate or change how the business is run. Additionally, fees can eat into profits, and the franchisor holds a significant amount of control.

Final Thoughts for Entrepreneurs

For aspiring entrepreneurs, a franchise contract can be a pathway to owning and operating a business with built-in brand recognition and support. But it's crucial to thoroughly understand the terms and conditions of the contract before committing. By carefully reviewing key clauses, such as fees, territory rights, and operational guidelines, you'll be better equipped to make an informed decision and succeed as a franchisee.

In the end, a franchise contract represents a partnership. While you gain the benefits of an established business model, you also take on the responsibility of maintaining the franchiser's brand reputation. Understanding the legal and operational aspects of the contract is key to ensuring your franchise journey is both profitable and rewarding.

Franchise Contracts vs. Building a Brand from Zero to Hero: A Comparison

For entrepreneurs, deciding whether to invest in a franchise or build a brand from scratch can be a tough call. Both paths come with their own advantages, challenges, and risks. Here, we'll break down the key differences between entering into a franchise contract and building your own brand from the ground up, giving you a clear idea of what to expect with each approach.

---

1. Brand Recognition and Trust

- **Franchise Contract:**
  When you invest in a franchise, you are essentially buying into an established brand. The name, logo, products, and reputation are already familiar to customers. This immediate brand recognition can be a major advantage, as it draws in customers who already know and trust the brand.

  Example: Opening a well-known fast-food chain like McDonald's will give you access to a loyal customer base from day one. The brand recognition is built-in.

- **Building a Brand from Zero:**
  Starting your own business means you have to build your brand from scratch. This takes time, effort, and a strong marketing strategy. You'll need to establish trust with

customers and create brand awareness before seeing significant growth.

Example: If you create a new local burger joint, you'll need to work on differentiating your brand, building customer loyalty, and standing out from competitors.

Verdict: A franchise gives you an immediate advantage with an established brand, whereas building a brand requires significant effort to gain recognition.

2. Startup Costs

- **Franchise Contract:**
  Franchises often come with upfront fees, including the franchise fee, training costs, and expenses for equipment, inventory, and setting up the business according to the franchisor's standards. While this can be expensive, the business model is already proven, reducing the overall risk.

  Example: A franchise fee for a popular brand can range from tens of thousands to even hundreds of thousands of dollars. Plus, you'll pay ongoing royalties.

- **Building a Brand from Zero:**
  Starting a business from scratch may have lower initial costs, depending on the type of business. You have the freedom to choose how much to spend on marketing,

branding, and setup. However, because the risk is higher, securing funding can be more difficult.

Example: You may need to bootstrap the business or take out loans to cover costs such as a location, marketing, and product development.

Verdict: While franchises often have high upfront costs, they come with a proven model. Building a brand can be less expensive initially, but it may require more investment over time to gain traction.

---

3. Control and Flexibility

- **Franchise Contract:**
  When you buy a franchise, you agree to operate within the franchisor's established framework. This means you must follow strict guidelines on how the business is run—everything from branding and marketing to pricing and product offerings is dictated by the franchisor. Your ability to innovate or change things up is limited.

  Example: If you own a fast-food franchise, you may not have the flexibility to introduce new menu items or change the store layout.

- **Building a Brand from Zero:**
  As a business owner starting from scratch, you have

complete control over every aspect of your business. You can develop your own products, set your prices, and create your marketing strategy. The downside is that the freedom comes with added responsibility, and there's a higher risk of failure.

Example: You can decide to pivot your business strategy, introduce new products, or completely re-brand if you feel it's necessary.

Verdict: A franchise provides structure but limits your control. Building a brand from scratch gives you full control but comes with more risks.

4. Support and Resources

- **Franchise Contract:**
  One of the biggest advantages of a franchise is the built-in support system. Most franchisors provide comprehensive training, ongoing support, and access to resources such as marketing tools, supply chains, and business management systems. This support reduces the learning curve for new entrepreneurs.

  Example: A franchisor might provide training on everything from day-to-day operations to customer service, as well as ongoing assistance to help you succeed.

- **Building a Brand from Zero:**
  When starting your own business, you won't have the luxury of a ready-made support system. You'll need to figure out every aspect of the business yourself—finding suppliers, managing marketing, and developing your own operational procedures. However, you can seek mentors, join business communities, or hire consultants to help guide you.

  Example: You'll have to build your own network of suppliers, learn the best marketing strategies, and handle every aspect of the business on your own.

  Verdict: Franchises offer strong support and resources, while starting from scratch requires building your own network and infrastructure.

---

5. Risk and Reward

- **Franchise Contract:**
  Franchising generally carries less risk than starting a new business. The franchisor has already tested and proven the business model, and there's usually an established customer base. However, because you pay ongoing royalties and fees, your profit margins may be lower than with an independent business.

Example: While you may have a steady stream of customers, the royalties you pay to the franchisor reduce your net income.

- **Building a Brand from Zero:**
  Starting your own business is riskier because there's no guarantee that your idea will work. However, the rewards can be much higher if you succeed. Since you own the brand outright, there are no royalties, and all the profits are yours to reinvest or pocket.

  Example: If your business takes off, you keep 100% of the profits, and your brand becomes your asset, which you can expand or sell in the future.

  Verdict: A franchise reduces risk but limits potential profits. Building a brand is riskier, but the potential rewards are greater.

6. Scalability

- **Franchise Contract:**
  Franchises are typically easier to scale, as the franchisor provides a blueprint for opening new locations. Once you've mastered the model, expanding to multiple locations can be relatively straightforward. However, your ability to innovate or differentiate your new locations may still be limited.

Example: A successful franchisee may open multiple outlets in different locations, following the same operational model.

- **Building a Brand from Zero:**
Scaling a business you built from scratch can be more difficult because you must develop the operational systems and processes yourself. However, you have full control over how you scale, whether it's through new product lines, locations, or market expansions.

Example: If your brand gains a strong following, you can expand in any direction—new locations, online presence, or even licensing your brand.

Verdict: Franchises offer an easier path to scaling, but with less control. Building a brand takes more effort to scale, but you can expand in any direction.

Final Thoughts

Choosing between a franchise and building a brand from scratch depends on your personality, goals, and risk tolerance as an entrepreneur. If you prefer a structured, lower-risk opportunity with built-in support and brand recognition, franchising may be the right choice. However, if you crave independence, control, and are willing to take on more risk for potentially greater rewards, building your own brand may be more appealing.

Both paths can lead to success, but understanding the pros and cons of each will help you make the best decision for your entrepreneurial journey. Whether you decide to follow a franchise model or create something entirely your own, the key is to be informed, prepared, and passionate about the business you're building.

Investment Contracts: Stocks, Trust Funds, and the CFD Trading Trap for Entrepreneurial Hopefuls

When it comes to investing, contracts play a crucial role in defining the rights and responsibilities of the involved parties. Whether you're dealing with stocks, trust funds, or high-risk ventures like CFD trading, understanding the underlying contractual obligations can save you from costly mistakes. In this section, we'll explore the different types of investment contracts, their potential benefits, and the traps that entrepreneurial hopefuls, especially those lured into speculative trading, should avoid.

1. Stock Investment Contracts

- **What They Are:**
A stock represents ownership in a company, and when you buy shares, you enter into a contract with that company. Stock contracts define the relationship between the shareholder (you) and the company, outlining your rights, such as voting rights, dividends, and the ability to transfer your shares.
- **Key Clauses:**
    - **Voting Rights:** As a shareholder, you may have the right to vote on certain company matters, like electing the board of directors.
    - **Dividends:** Some stocks entitle you to a portion of the company's profits, known as dividends, which are paid out periodically.
    - **Share Transferability:** Contracts often detail how easily you can sell or transfer your shares on the stock market.
- **Why It Matters:**
Stock investments are generally considered to be relatively safe compared to more speculative ventures. The risk varies depending on the company's performance, but you can mitigate risk by diversifying your stock portfolio and investing in well-established companies.

Example: If you purchase shares in a Fortune 500 company, you're entering into a relatively straightforward contract that gives you a small slice of ownership in a stable company.

Verdict: Stock investment contracts are a common and secure way to grow wealth, as long as you understand the terms and invest wisely.

---

2. Trust Fund Contracts

- **What They Are:**
  A trust fund is a legal entity where assets are held for the benefit of specific individuals or organizations. The contract governing the trust outlines the terms under which the assets will be managed, distributed, and potentially grown. Trusts are often used to manage wealth, secure financial futures, or ensure that assets are properly distributed after death.
- **Key Clauses:**
    - **Trustee Responsibilities:** The trustee is responsible for managing the assets in the trust according to the contract. This may include investing funds, paying out income, or distributing assets to beneficiaries.
    - **Beneficiary Rights:** The beneficiaries are the people entitled to receive the trust's assets. The contract outlines when and how the assets will be distributed (e.g., when a beneficiary reaches a certain age).
    - **Duration of the Trust:** Some trusts are temporary, while others are designed to last for generations. The

contract specifies the lifespan of the trust and the conditions under which it may end.
- **Why It Matters:**
Trust fund contracts offer a structured way to manage wealth and protect assets. They are ideal for estate planning or ensuring financial security for future generations. However, the legal complexity requires a good understanding of the terms, and it's advisable to seek professional guidance.

Example: A family trust may be set up to manage assets for children until they reach adulthood, with the trustee responsible for investing and growing those assets in the meantime.

Verdict: Trust fund contracts are ideal for long-term wealth management but require careful planning and the right expertise to execute effectively.

---

3. The CFD Trading Trap for Entrepreneurial Hopefuls

- **What They Are:**
Contracts for Difference (CFDs) are speculative investment contracts where traders bet on the price movement of an asset (like stocks, commodities, or currencies) without actually owning the asset. The contract is between you and

the broker, and you make a profit or loss based on whether the asset's price moves in the direction you predicted.
- **Key Clauses:**
  - **Leverage and Margin:** CFDs often allow you to trade on margin, meaning you can control a large position with a small amount of capital. However, this also means you can lose more than your initial investment if the market moves against you.
  - **Fees and Costs:** CFD trading often comes with hidden fees, such as overnight holding costs, spreads, and commissions. These costs can eat into any profits you make.
  - **Risk Disclosures:** Most CFD contracts include warnings about the high-risk nature of this type of trading, but these are often overlooked by traders who focus on potential gains.
- **Why It Matters:**
CFD trading is notoriously risky, and it's easy for entrepreneurial hopefuls to get lured into it by promises of quick returns. However, many people underestimate the volatility and leverage involved. In reality, a significant percentage of CFD traders lose money, and the contracts are designed in such a way that even small market fluctuations can lead to huge losses.

Example: You may think you're making a smart investment by betting on the price of oil through a CFD. But a small, unexpected price movement in the opposite direction could wipe out your account due to the leverage involved.

Verdict: CFDs are a high-risk investment that should be approached with extreme caution. For most entrepreneurs, especially those new to the market, traditional investments like stocks or mutual funds are a safer bet.

Comparing the Investment Types

Type	Risk Level	Potential Reward	Control Over Assets	Time Horizon	Complexity
Stocks	Moderate	Moderate to High	Direct control of shares	Medium to Long-Term	Low to Moderate
Trust Funds	Low	Moderate	Indirect (via trustee)	Long-Term	High
CFD Trading	High	High (but mostly losses)	No ownership of assets	Short-Term	Very High

Final Thoughts: Entrepreneurs Beware

While stocks and trust funds can be valuable tools for growing wealth, CFD trading is fraught with danger, especially for those without experience. Entrepreneurs should be cautious when entering high-risk contracts that promise fast profits, as they often lead to quick losses instead.

Stocks offer a relatively secure way to invest and grow capital, while trust funds provide a method for protecting and managing wealth

Tech Bros and Startup Foundations: A Lawyer's Perspective

For every tech enthusiast aspiring to become the next Bill Gates or Elon Musk, it's crucial to understand that building a successful startup is not just about having a groundbreaking idea or killer code. It's about laying a solid legal and operational foundation from the very start. As a lawyer, guiding tech entrepreneurs through this process involves setting up the necessary structures to protect their interests, ensure compliance, and foster long-term growth.

Here's a breakdown of the legal essentials every tech startup founder needs to consider:

1. Business Entity Formation: LLC or Corporation?

- **Why It Matters:**
  The choice of business entity will impact your startup's taxation, liability protection, and ability to attract investors. Most tech startups choose either a Limited Liability Company (LLC) or a corporation (often a C-Corp or S-Corp), depending on their long-term goals.
- **LLC vs. Corporation:**
  - **LLC:** Offers flexibility in management and taxation, making it a good choice for early-stage startups. Owners (members) aren't personally liable for business debts, providing some protection.
  - **C-Corporation:** Ideal for startups seeking outside investors, especially venture capitalists. It offers the ability to issue stock and attracts larger investments, but it comes with double taxation (tax on the company's income and on shareholders' dividends).
  - **S-Corporation:** Similar to a C-Corp but avoids double taxation by passing income directly to shareholders. However, it has more restrictions on ownership and shareholding.

  Pro Tip: If your goal is rapid growth and external funding, a C-Corp is the way to go, especially in tech-heavy ecosystems like Silicon Valley. But, for bootstrapped ventures, an LLC might suffice until you scale up.

2. Intellectual Property (IP) Protection: Safeguard Your Innovation

- **Why It Matters:**
  In tech, intellectual property is often the most valuable asset. Failing to protect it early on can lead to devastating consequences—like someone else copying or exploiting your ideas.
- **Steps to Protect IP:**
  - **Patents:** If your startup involves novel technology or processes, patenting your invention can prevent others from using or selling your innovation without permission.
  - **Trademarks:** Registering your company name, logo, or slogan as a trademark protects your brand identity.
  - **Copyrights:** For software startups, copyrights protect the source code you develop.
  - **Trade Secrets:** For algorithms, processes, or data that give you a competitive edge, ensure they are legally protected as trade secrets.

  Pro Tip: Don't delay protecting your intellectual property—filing for patents and trademarks early can prevent future legal headaches and investor hesitance.

3. Founders' Agreement: Clarify Roles and Ownership

- **Why It Matters:**
  Many startups fail because of co-founder disputes. A well-drafted founders' agreement ensures everyone is on the same page from day one. It outlines each founder's roles, responsibilities, ownership stakes, and what happens in cases of disputes or exit.
- **Key Clauses:**
  - **Equity Ownership:** Define who owns what percentage of the company and under what terms.
  - **Vesting Schedule:** Protect the company by implementing a vesting schedule. This ensures that founders only earn their equity over time (e.g., 4 years with a 1-year cliff), preventing a co-founder from walking away with a large equity share early on.
  - **Roles and Responsibilities:** Clearly outline each founder's role in the company to avoid power struggles or miscommunication later.
  - **Dispute Resolution:** Detail how disputes will be resolved, whether through mediation, arbitration, or other means.

Pro Tip: Include vesting schedules and conflict resolution mechanisms to prevent costly legal battles down the road.

---

4. Contracts with Employees and Contractors

- **Why It Matters:**
  Startups often grow quickly, and ensuring that every employee and contractor is legally bound to the company is essential. You'll need robust contracts to define work expectations, protect intellectual property, and prevent future disputes.
- **Key Contracts:**
  - **Employment Contracts:** Define job roles, compensation, and terms of employment. Ensure non-disclosure and non-compete agreements are included where appropriate.
  - **Contractor Agreements:** For freelancers or contractors, make sure there's a clear agreement that they don't own the IP they create—this belongs to the company.
  - **Invention Assignment Agreements:** These agreements ensure that anything created by an employee or contractor related to the business is owned by the company, not the individual.

  Pro Tip: Every person who touches your startup should sign an NDA and an invention assignment agreement to prevent future ownership disputes.

---

5. Funding and Investor Agreements: Navigating Term Sheets and Equity Deals

- **Why It Matters:**
Bringing on investors can supercharge your growth, but it's vital to know what you're signing up for. Investor agreements, term sheets, and equity deals all have long-term implications for control and ownership.
- **Key Considerations:**
    - **Equity vs. Debt Financing:** Decide whether to raise money by giving up equity (ownership) or taking on debt (loans). Equity deals often involve giving investors a stake in the company, which means a portion of profits and decision-making power.
    - **Preferred Stock:** Many investors will ask for preferred stock, giving them rights over common shareholders, like getting paid first in case of liquidation.
    - **Dilution:** Understand that raising money can dilute the founders' ownership percentage, meaning you'll own a smaller slice of a larger pie.

Pro Tip: Negotiate the terms carefully, especially when it comes to liquidation preferences and voting rights. A bad investor deal can leave you with little control over your company.

---

6. Compliance and Regulatory Requirements: Don't Get Caught Off Guard

- **Why It Matters:**
  Tech startups often operate in highly regulated environments, especially if they deal with data, health tech, or financial services. Failing to comply with industry regulations can lead to lawsuits, fines, or even the shutdown of your business.
- **Key Compliance Areas:**
  - **Data Privacy:** Ensure compliance with data protection laws like the GDPR or CCPA if you handle user data.
  - **Health Tech Regulations:** If you're in the medical field, comply with healthcare privacy laws like HIPAA.
  - **Securities Laws:** If you're raising money from investors, make sure you comply with securities regulations to avoid penalties or lawsuits.

  Pro Tip: Get legal advice specific to your industry's regulations early to avoid costly compliance mistakes.

---

7. Exit Strategy: Plan for the Future

- **Why It Matters:**
  Every founder dream of an exit, whether it's through acquisition, IPO, or another way of cashing out. Planning for your exit strategy early helps shape how you grow the company.
- **Types of Exits:**

- **Acquisition:** A larger company may acquire your startup, which can be lucrative if done right. Ensure your contracts and IP are in order to make the company attractive for acquisition.
- **IPO (Initial Public Offering):** If your startup reaches a significant size, you may take it public and sell shares to the general public.
- **Merger:** Sometimes startups merge with other companies to achieve greater market share or technological advancement.

Pro Tip: Make sure your contracts, financials, and intellectual property are clean and organized to attract potential buyers or investors when the time comes.

Final Thoughts: Legal First, Code Later

For tech entrepreneurs dreaming of becoming the next big name in the industry, the most valuable advice is this: **get your legal foundation right from the start**. While code and innovation are vital, the framework that supports your startup—contracts, IP protections, and legal agreements—will determine how scalable, secure, and successful your business will become.

By partnering with a good legal advisor early on, you'll avoid pitfalls, protect your assets, and pave the way for sustainable growth. After all, the right legal foundation is just as important as that next great idea!

Understanding Common Clauses in Layman's Terms:

- **Indemnity:** This means that one party agrees to compensate the other for any losses or damages they cause. For example, if a tenant damages the landlord's property, the indemnity clause might require the tenant to pay for repairs.

- **Force Majeure:** This refers to unexpected events (like natural disasters) that could prevent one or both parties from fulfilling their contract. This clause usually excuses the affected party from liability.

- **Governing Law:** This clause states which jurisdiction's laws will apply to interpret and enforce the contract. For example, if you're signing a contract in California, the governing law might be California state law.

- **Entire Agreement:** This means that the written contract is the final word on the agreement between the parties, and any previous verbal or written agreements are not considered binding.

Written contracts are crucial for clearly defining the rights and responsibilities of all parties involved. Understanding these common clauses helps ensure that you know what you're agreeing to before signing on the dotted line.

Great! Let's dive into Chapter 3 on public law, starting with a focus on tax laws, criminal law, traffic laws, citizenship, and other related subjects. Here's a draft introduction to the chapter:

Chapter 3: Public Law and Its Reach into Everyday Life

Public law governs the relationships between individuals and the state, regulating the duties we owe to our governments and the rights we expect in return. From paying taxes to obeying traffic laws and understanding citizenship rights, public law plays a crucial role in maintaining social order and ensuring that the state functions smoothly. This chapter will delve into the most essential areas of public law, focusing on topics like tax laws, criminal justice, traffic regulations, and citizenship.

Public law touches every part of our daily lives, often without us noticing. Whether you're filing taxes, driving to work, or even establishing your legal residency, public law shapes the framework within which these activities take place. As we explore these topics, the aim is to make them approachable, ensuring you understand how they function, why they matter, and how they apply to you.

Criminal Law for the laymen:

Criminal law serves as one of the most fundamental pillars of public law, and its purpose extends beyond merely punishing wrongdoers. It's a carefully designed mechanism for maintaining order, protecting society, and ensuring justice for victims. But understanding criminal law in its full depth requires us to explore not only its legal aspects but also its connection to criminology and psychology.

Criminology provides insights into the causes and conditions of criminal behavior. It delves into factors such as socio-economic conditions, psychological predispositions, peer influence, and environmental factors, helping us understand why individuals may turn to crime. Criminal law, in turn, creates the framework for addressing these behaviors and preventing harm.

From a psychological perspective, criminal law also takes into account the mental state and intent of an individual at the time of the crime, commonly known as *mens rea* (the guilty mind). For instance, courts distinguish between crimes committed intentionally, recklessly, or negligently. This distinction is key because the law isn't just concerned with what a person did but also with *why* they did it.

1. **Actus Reus and Mens Rea**
   Criminal law is based on two primary elements: *actus reus* (the physical act of committing a crime) and *mens rea* (the mental intent behind it). For a crime to exist, there must

typically be both a wrongful act and a corresponding guilty mind. For example, if someone takes another's property but mistakenly believes it to be theirs, the lack of *mens rea* could serve as a defense.

2. **Crimes Against the Person vs. Crimes Against Property**
Criminal law is usually divided into two broad categories: crimes against individuals (e.g., assault, homicide) and crimes against property (e.g., theft, vandalism). Crimes against the person typically carry harsher penalties, reflecting the greater harm done to human life and well-being.

3. **Defenses to Criminal Charges**
Criminal defenses often tie into psychological elements. For instance, insanity, diminished responsibility, and intoxication are defenses that can mitigate or eliminate culpability. They focus on the defendant's mental state, suggesting that they may not have had the mental capacity to understand their actions.

4. **Rehabilitation vs. Punishment**
Modern criminal justice systems often wrestle with the balance between punishment and rehabilitation. From a psychological standpoint, the aim is not only to punish the offender but also to rehabilitate them to reduce recidivism. This understanding is crucial in shaping how laws are structured and enforced.

In sum, criminal law is about more than simply enforcing rules. It's an intersection of law, psychology, and society that seeks to balance punishment, protection, and prevention by understanding the deeper causes of criminal behavior. As we dig deeper into this chapter, we'll further explore these themes and the intricacies of how criminal law impacts society.

Philosophy of Crime and Punishment

Crime and punishment are central concerns of any legal system, and the way society views both has evolved over centuries. Philosophically, these concepts are tied to fundamental questions about human behavior, justice, morality, and the role of the state. Different schools of thought have tried to answer why we punish people for certain behaviors, and why some acts are considered crimes in the first place.

1. **Retribution**
   One of the oldest philosophies behind punishment is retribution. This idea stems from the belief that when someone commits a crime, they deserve to be punished in proportion to the harm they caused. It's essentially a form of moral balancing—the concept of *an eye for an eye*. Retribution focuses on the past act, aiming to exact justice for the wrong committed.
2. **Deterrence**
   Deterrence aims to prevent crime before it happens by making an example of offenders. There are two forms:

specific deterrence (discouraging the individual offender from committing more crimes) and *general deterrence* (sending a message to society at large that certain actions will have severe consequences). This philosophy is future-oriented, focusing on reducing the likelihood of crime through fear of punishment.

3. **Rehabilitation**

   Rehabilitation is centered on the idea that individuals can change, and the criminal justice system should help offenders reintegrate into society. This approach looks beyond punishment to address the root causes of criminal behavior, such as addiction, mental illness, or lack of education. It aims to transform the offender into a law-abiding citizen.

4. **Restorative Justice**

   Restorative justice emphasizes repairing the harm caused by criminal behavior. It often involves mediation between the victim and the offender, with the goal of reaching a solution that helps both parties. This approach focuses on healing rather than punishment, aiming to restore social balance and personal relationships.

5. **Incapacitation**

   Incapacitation seeks to protect society by removing dangerous individuals from the general population, either through imprisonment or, in extreme cases, capital punishment. The focus here is on public safety rather than moral judgment or the potential for rehabilitation.

Types of Crimes and Why They Are Punished

Crimes can generally be grouped into categories based on the harm they cause or the values they violate. The reason for punishment varies by the type of crime, but all aim to uphold the moral fabric of society, maintain order, and protect citizens.

1. **Crimes Against the Person**
   These crimes directly harm an individual, including assault, murder, rape, and kidnapping. Society punishes these crimes to protect the sanctity of human life and personal safety. Retribution and incapacitation are common reasons for punishing violent offenders, as society views them as dangerous and morally culpable.
2. **Crimes Against Property**
   Crimes like theft, burglary, and vandalism involve the unlawful taking or damaging of someone else's property. Punishment here serves to deter others from infringing on property rights, which are essential for economic stability and personal freedom. Restitution (returning stolen goods or paying for damages) is often part of the punishment.
3. **White-Collar Crimes**
   Fraud, embezzlement, insider trading, and bribery are examples of white-collar crimes. Though they may not involve physical harm, these crimes erode trust in institutions and cause financial devastation. Punishing these crimes serves to deter corporate wrongdoing and ensure fairness in business practices.
4. **Crimes Against the State**
   Treason, espionage, and terrorism are considered crimes against the state. These acts threaten national security and

the very foundation of the legal and political system. Punishment for such crimes is often severe, as their impact is far-reaching and threatens public safety on a large scale.
5. **Victimless Crimes**
   These include drug use, gambling, and prostitution, where the harm is considered to be more abstract or self-inflicted. The philosophy behind punishing these crimes is often debated. Some argue it's about maintaining social order or morality, while others see it as government overreach into personal freedom.
6. **Regulatory Crimes**
   Certain laws, like traffic laws or environmental regulations, exist to protect public welfare. Violating these may not cause immediate harm, but they increase the risk of accidents, public health issues, or environmental damage. Punishment in these cases often serves to deter negligence and maintain public safety.

The Intersection of Crime and Punishment

At its core, the philosophy of crime and punishment is about balancing the rights of individuals with the need to maintain a functioning society. Each type of crime challenges societal values in a different way, and each form of punishment aims to correct, prevent, or compensate for those harms. From a psychological and sociological perspective, punishment is as much about reinforcing societal norms as it is about individual accountability.

In summary, society punishes crimes to maintain order, protect citizens, and promote justice. The type of crime—whether it's a violent act, theft, corporate fraud, or regulatory violation—determines the rationale behind the punishment, be it deterrence, retribution, rehabilitation, or incapacitation.

Criminal Procedure Law and Its Importance

Criminal procedure law governs the process by which crimes are investigated, prosecuted, adjudicated, and punished. It is a vital component of the justice system because it outlines the rules that ensure the fair treatment of individuals, the protection of their rights, and the maintenance of public order. These rules guide everything from the initial investigation of a crime to the final verdict, and they exist to balance the powers of the state with the rights of the accused.

1. *Due Process and Fair Treatment*

One of the most fundamental reasons criminal procedure laws is important is that it ensures **due process**, which refers to the fair treatment of individuals within the justice system. This principle ensures that everyone receives a fair trial, regardless of the crime they are accused of, their background, or their status. Without criminal procedure laws in place, the risk of arbitrary detention, unfair trials, and wrongful convictions would be much higher.

Key elements of due process include:

- The right to a fair trial.
- The right to be informed of the charges.
- The right to legal representation.
- The right to a speedy trial.
- The right to confront witnesses.
- The right against self-incrimination.

These principles prevent the state from abusing its power and protect individuals from the potential unfairness of the system.

2. **Rights of the Accused**

Criminal procedure law also lays out **specific rights** that the accused have throughout the criminal process. These rights are crucial in preventing innocent individuals from being wrongly convicted and ensuring that guilty parties are treated justly.

Some of the most important rights include:

- **The right to remain silent**: This is protected under the principle of "no self-incrimination." Defendants are not required to testify against themselves, which prevents the prosecution from coercing confessions.
- **The right to legal representation**: Everyone accused of a crime has the right to have a lawyer, and if they cannot afford one, the state must provide one. This ensures that even those without financial resources have the opportunity to defend themselves adequately.
- **Protection against double jeopardy**: Individuals cannot be tried twice for the same crime, ensuring that once acquitted, they cannot be prosecuted again for the same incident.

- **The right to bail**: In many systems, individuals have the right to be released on bail before trial, ensuring they are not unjustly held in custody for long periods.

3. Ensuring Lawful Investigation

Criminal procedure law also dictates how **investigations** should be conducted to ensure they are lawful and respect the rights of individuals. For example, law enforcement must follow specific procedures when arresting suspects, gathering evidence, and conducting interrogations. Without these rules, there could be unchecked abuse by police or investigators.

Important procedural rules in criminal investigations include:

- **Warrants for search and seizure**: Law enforcement must often obtain a court-issued warrant to search private property, ensuring that citizens' privacy rights are protected.
- **Probable cause**: Before making an arrest or conducting a search, police must have reasonable grounds to believe that a crime has been committed.
- **Miranda rights**: In many jurisdictions, police must inform suspects of their rights (such as the right to remain silent and the right to an attorney) when they are arrested or questioned.

If law enforcement violates these procedural rules, any evidence obtained may be inadmissible in court, safeguarding individuals from illegal practices.

4. Maintaining Public Order and Accountability

Criminal procedure law is not just about protecting the rights of the accused; it also plays a role in maintaining **public order**. By ensuring that criminal cases are handled fairly and transparently, it reinforces public trust in the justice system. People need to know that those who commit crimes will be held accountable in a just manner.

Procedural law holds law enforcement, prosecutors, and even the judiciary accountable. It ensures that power is not abused and that every step in the criminal process, from arrest to sentencing, is conducted according to established laws and guidelines.

5. The Trial Process and Justice

Criminal procedure law outlines the rules for **criminal trials**, which are the core of the justice system. Trials provide an opportunity for the facts of a case to be presented, for both the prosecution and defense to argue their case, and for a neutral party (a judge or jury) to make a decision based on the evidence.

Some of the key aspects of criminal trials include:

- **The right to a jury trial**: In many systems, individuals have the right to be judged by a jury of their peers.
- **The burden of proof**: The prosecution bears the burden of proving the defendant's guilt beyond a reasonable doubt.
- **Cross-examination**: Both parties have the right to question witnesses to ensure that testimony is reliable and truthful.

Without these trial procedures, the risk of injustice would increase, as trials could become one-sided or manipulated.

6. Appeals and Post-Conviction Remedies

Criminal procedure law also provides mechanisms for **appeals** and **post-conviction remedies**. If a defendant believes that a mistake was made during their trial, they have the right to appeal to a higher court.

This is crucial for ensuring that errors in legal interpretation or procedure can be corrected, preventing miscarriages of justice.

Constitutional Law and Administrative Law and Their Relationship with Criminal Justice:

Constitutional law and administrative law are two fundamental branches of public law that play a critical role in shaping the legal landscape. Both serve as the backbone of government authority and the protection of individual rights, but they operate in different spheres. Constitutional law focuses on the structure and principles that define a nation's governance, while administrative law governs how laws are implemented and enforced by various public authorities.

In this chapter, we will explore these two areas, discuss their intersection, and connect them to the roles of the prosecutor in administrative law, as well as how constitutional law ties into criminal law and criminal procedure.

1. What Is Constitutional Law?

Constitutional law is the body of law that defines the structure and powers of the government and the rights of individuals in relation to the state. At its core, it encompasses:

- The **constitution** of the state, which outlines the framework for government powers.
- The **separation of powers** among the branches of government (executive, legislative, judicial).

- The **rule of law**, which ensures that all actions of government are subject to legal principles.
- The **protection of fundamental rights** such as freedom of speech, the right to due process, and equal protection under the law.

Constitutional law sets the legal limits within which governments can operate, ensuring that their power is not abused and that individual rights are respected. It forms the foundation upon which all other laws, including criminal law, are built.

2. What Is Administrative Law?

Administrative law governs the activities of government agencies and public officials. It ensures that government actions are lawful, reasonable, and fair by providing rules and procedures that these bodies must follow. This area of law covers:

- **Regulatory agencies** that oversee everything from public health to environmental protection.
- **Licensing authorities** that issue permits and licenses for businesses and professionals.
- **Disciplinary bodies** that enforce standards in various professions.
- **Public services** such as education, healthcare, and housing, ensuring they are delivered lawfully and equitably.

Administrative law helps maintain government accountability by providing a framework for individuals and businesses to challenge decisions made by public authorities if they believe their rights have been violated.

3. Constitutional Law and Criminal Law

Constitutional law plays a central role in shaping criminal law and criminal procedure. The key principles of constitutional law directly impact how criminal cases are handled, including:

- **Due process**: This constitutional principle ensures that individuals accused of crimes are treated fairly and justly. It requires that the legal processes followed in criminal cases are consistent and transparent.
- **Presumption of innocence**: Stemming from constitutional protections, individuals are presumed innocent until proven guilty beyond a reasonable doubt. This principle underpins the fairness of criminal trials.
- **Right to a fair trial**: The constitution guarantees that individuals have the right to defend themselves in court, have access to legal representation, and present evidence in their favor.
- **Protection against self-incrimination**: Individuals cannot be forced to testify against themselves, a right enshrined in many constitutions. This ties directly into the right to remain silent, which plays a key role in criminal procedures.
- **Equal protection under the law**: Criminal law must be applied equally to all, regardless of an individual's race, gender, or socioeconomic status. The constitution ensures that no one is above the law and that everyone receives equal treatment in the criminal justice system.

In this way, constitutional law provides a framework that safeguards individuals from abuses of state power in the criminal process. It ensures that justice is not only served but done so in a manner consistent with the highest legal standards.

4. Criminal Procedure and Constitutional Law

Criminal procedure refers to the rules governing how criminal cases are processed from investigation to trial. Constitutional protections are embedded in these procedures to prevent arbitrary use of state power. Key areas where constitutional law intersects with criminal procedure include:

- **Search and seizure**: The constitution often protects individuals from unreasonable searches and seizures by law enforcement. This means that authorities must have a valid warrant or probable cause before conducting a search.
- **Arrests and detentions**: Constitutional law ensures that individuals cannot be arbitrarily arrested or detained without justification. Legal standards for issuing arrest warrants, as well as the right to challenge unlawful detention, are constitutionally guaranteed.
- **Right to counsel**: Individuals accused of crimes have the right to legal representation. In cases where a defendant cannot afford a lawyer, the state may be required to provide one.
- **Speedy trial**: The constitution often requires that criminal cases are handled in a timely manner, preventing excessive delays that could unfairly prejudice the accused.

These procedural safeguards ensure that criminal justice operates fairly, providing both accountability for wrongdoing and protection of individual rights. Without the guiding principles of constitutional law, criminal procedures could become arbitrary, leading to potential abuses of power.

Taxation Law for The Laymen:

Taxation law is one of the cornerstones of public law, governing the rules and processes by which governments impose and collect taxes. Taxes are essential for funding public services, infrastructure, education, healthcare, and other vital components that help societies function smoothly. In this chapter, we'll delve into how taxation law works, the types of taxes, and the principles behind them, providing an understanding of the tax obligations individuals and businesses face and how these obligations are enforced by law.

1. What Is Taxation Law?

Taxation law refers to the body of legal rules and regulations that govern the collection of taxes by governmental authorities. It outlines:

- **Who must pay taxes** (individuals, corporations, organizations).
- **What types of taxes** are owed (income tax, property tax, corporate tax, etc.).
- **How taxes are calculated**, collected, and enforced.

Taxation law also specifies the consequences for failing to meet tax obligations, including penalties, fines, and legal actions. The underlying purpose of taxation law is to ensure the fair and efficient collection of taxes, which are used to fund public goods and services.

2. Types of Taxes

There are several different types of taxes that individuals and businesses may be subject to. Some of the most common include:

- **Income Tax**: This is a tax on the income earned by individuals and businesses. In most jurisdictions, income taxes are progressive, meaning that higher earners pay a larger percentage of their income in taxes. Governments rely on income tax to fund many of their operations.

- **Corporate Tax**: Similar to income tax but applied to companies, corporate taxes are levied on the profits of businesses. The rate of taxation can vary depending on the country or region, and corporations often have legal and accounting strategies to manage their tax liabilities.

- **Sales Tax / Value Added Tax (VAT)**: A consumption tax imposed on the sale of goods and services. In many regions, VAT is applied at every stage of production and distribution, and the final consumer bears the cost.

- **Property Tax**: Owners of land and buildings are often required to pay property taxes, which are typically used to fund local governments, such as municipalities and counties, for services like schools, fire departments, and road maintenance.

- **Excise Tax**: A tax on specific goods, like fuel, tobacco, and alcohol. Excise taxes are often designed not only to generate revenue but also to discourage the consumption of certain products deemed harmful to society.

- **Capital Gains Tax**: A tax on the profits made from the sale of assets such as stocks, bonds, or real estate. Capital gains tax is generally lower than income tax, encouraging investment but still ensuring some revenue is captured from profitable transactions.

3. Principles of Taxation

Several key principles guide the design and implementation of tax laws. These principles are intended to ensure that taxes are fair, transparent, and effective.

- **Equity**: Tax systems should aim to distribute the tax burden fairly. This is often reflected in **progressive taxation**, where those with greater financial means contribute a higher percentage of their income to taxes.
- **Efficiency**: Taxes should be collected in a way that does not create undue economic distortion. For example, excessive taxation on business profits may discourage investment, which can harm economic growth.
- **Certainty**: Taxpayers should be able to predict how much tax they will owe, based on clear and consistent rules. A tax system that is too complex or arbitrary can create uncertainty, making it difficult for businesses and individuals to plan their financial futures.
- **Convenience**: The process of paying taxes should be as simple and convenient as possible. Systems like payroll deductions or online tax filing are examples of efforts to make tax payment easier for taxpayers.
- **Revenue Sufficiency**: The primary goal of taxation is to raise enough revenue to fund government operations and public services. Tax policies must strike a balance between raising enough revenue and not overburdening the economy.

4. Tax Evasion vs. Tax Avoidance

Taxation law is also concerned with the distinction between **tax evasion** and **tax avoidance**. While both involve efforts to reduce the amount of taxes paid, there is a critical legal distinction between the two.

- **Tax Evasion**: This is illegal and involves intentionally misreporting or hiding income, assets, or transactions to reduce tax liability. Tax evasion can result in significant penalties, including fines and imprisonment.
- **Tax Avoidance**: This refers to the legal use of tax loopholes, deductions, and credits to minimize tax liabilities. While legal, excessive tax avoidance can lead to changes in tax laws to close unintended loopholes.

5. Tax Audits and Enforcement

Tax laws include mechanisms for enforcement to ensure compliance. Governments use various methods to audit individuals and businesses suspected of not fully complying with tax laws. An **audit** is a detailed examination of tax filings, and if discrepancies are found, taxpayers may face penalties.

In some cases, tax disputes may escalate to court, where a judge or tax tribunal will decide whether the tax authority's claim is justified. For businesses, tax compliance is particularly important, as tax disputes can lead to reputational damage and financial loss.

6. How Taxes Affect Business and Investment

Taxes play a significant role in influencing business decisions. For entrepreneurs and investors, understanding tax laws is crucial to making informed financial decisions. Businesses must account for taxes in their cost structures and strategic planning, as different tax rates can significantly impact profitability. Additionally, tax incentives such as deductions for research and development, investment in certain sectors, or the creation of jobs can encourage businesses to engage in activities that align with public policy goals.

Tax laws are also key for international businesses. Corporations operating in multiple countries must navigate **international tax laws**, including **transfer pricing** (how profits are allocated across countries) and **double taxation treaties** (which prevent companies from being taxed twice on the same income).

7. The Role of Tax Professionals

Given the complexity of tax laws, many individuals and businesses seek the help of **tax professionals**, including accountants, tax attorneys, and consultants, to ensure compliance and optimize tax outcomes. These professionals can help with tax planning, filing returns, and representing taxpayers in disputes with tax authorities.

Tax professionals are particularly important for businesses, as tax mistakes can result in significant financial penalties and legal challenges. For this reason, it's critical to consult with qualified professionals to navigate the maze of tax regulations effectively.

Chapter 4: Corporate Law—An Intersection of Civil Law and Public Law

Corporate law stands as a unique blend of civil law and public law, combining principles from both areas to regulate the formation, governance, and operation of businesses while ensuring they comply with public standards. It plays a crucial role in managing the relationship between private entities and the public good, with aspects drawn from contract law, tort law, and regulatory oversight.

Civil Law in Corporate Law

At its core, corporate law is built upon civil law principles. These govern the relationships between individuals and corporations, including agreements made between shareholders, directors, employees, and other parties. Key civil law concepts in corporate law include:

- **Contracts**: Corporations regularly engage in contracts, whether with suppliers, clients, or employees. The rights and obligations between these parties are governed by contract law, a sub-branch of civil law.
- **Liability**: Directors and shareholders have duties outlined in civil law, such as fiduciary responsibilities, that may expose them to personal liability if breached.
- **Dispute Resolution**: Civil law provides the mechanisms for resolving disputes within the corporate context, such as breach of contract or tortious claims like negligence.

Public Law in Corporate Law

Public law regulates how corporations interact with the state and society. It establishes frameworks for ensuring companies operate within legal boundaries that protect the public interest. Some areas of public law within corporate law include:

- **Regulatory Compliance**: Corporations must comply with a range of regulations, from environmental standards to labor laws, ensuring that their operations are not harmful to the public.
- **Tax Law**: Corporations are subject to tax obligations that are dictated by public law. Governments impose taxes to generate revenue, and

corporations are often involved in complex tax planning to ensure compliance while minimizing liability.
- **Antitrust Law**: Public law limits the extent to which corporations can dominate a market or form monopolies, ensuring competition and preventing abuse of power.

How Corporate Law Bridges Civil and Public Law

Corporate law acts as a mediator between private business interests and the public welfare. It allows companies to engage in contracts, make profits, and grow while also being bound by public law rules that ensure transparency, accountability, and fair practices. For example, a company may have a civil law-based duty to honor its contracts but also a public law obligation to adhere to regulations concerning environmental protection or consumer rights.

- **Example: Mergers and Acquisitions**: When two companies decide to merge, the transaction is governed by civil law principles such as contract law. However, they must also meet public law obligations, including antitrust reviews by government agencies to ensure the merger doesn't stifle competition.

- **Example: Employment Law**: Civil law governs the terms of employment contracts, while public law dictates the broader labor standards companies must adhere to, such as minimum wage laws, workplace safety regulations, and anti-discrimination policies.

By balancing the needs of businesses to operate freely with the necessity of protecting the public, corporate law creates an ecosystem where businesses can flourish while safeguarding societal interests. Understanding this blend of civil and public law is essential for corporate actors and legal professionals to navigate the legal landscape effectively.

Chapter 5: Understanding Legal Terminology

Now that we've laid the groundwork for understanding how the law operates and how the state functions to regulate society, it's important to get familiar with some key legal terms. These terms are commonly used in legal discussions, and grasping them will help you better understand the inner workings of the law. You can find an extensive list of these terms on the United States Courts website, but I'll simplify and format them here for easy reading.

In the upcoming section, it's essential for readers to become familiar with common legal terminology, as this will strengthen their understanding of the legal system. Rather than diving deep into legal jargon, this chapter will introduce key terms that are frequently used in courtrooms, contracts, and legal proceedings in a way that's easy to grasp for laymen. By breaking down complex legal language into simple explanations, readers will be better equipped to interpret laws, rights, and obligations within different contexts.

Below is a list of terms, reformatted for clarity, that can be found in the United States Courts Glossary:

A

Acquittal	A jury verdict that a criminal defendant is not guilty, or the finding of a judge that the evidence is insufficient to support a conviction.
Active judge	A judge in the full-time service of the court. Compare to senior judge.
Administrative Office of the United States Courts (AO)	The federal agency responsible for collecting court statistics, administering the federal courts' budget, and performing many other administrative and programmatic functions, under the direction and supervision of the

	Judicial Conference of the United States.
Admissible	A term used to describe evidence that may be considered by a jury or judge in civil and criminal cases.
Adversary proceeding	A lawsuit arising in or related to a bankruptcy case that begins by filing a complaint with the court, that is, a "trial" that takes place within the context of a bankruptcy case.
Affidavit/Sworn statement	A written or printed statement made under oath.
Affirmed	In the practice of the court of appeals, it means that the court of appeals has concluded that the lower court decision is correct and will stand as rendered by the lower court.
Alternate juror	A juror selected in the same manner as a regular juror who hears all the evidence but does not help decide the case unless called on to replace a regular juror.
Alternative dispute resolution (ADR)	A procedure for settling a dispute outside the courtroom. Most forms of ADR are not binding, and involve referral of the case to a neutral party

	such as an arbitrator or mediator.
Amicus curiae	Latin for "friend of the court." It is advice formally offered to the court in a brief filed by an entity interested in, but not a party to, the case.
Answer	The formal written statement by a defendant in a civil case that responds to a complaint, articulating the grounds for defense.
Appeal	A request made after a trial by a party that has lost on one or more issues that a higher court review the decision to determine if it was correct. To make such a request is "to appeal" or "to take an appeal." One who appeals is called the "appellant;" the other party is the "appellee."
Appellant	The party who appeals a district court's decision, usually seeking reversal of that decision.
Appellate	About appeals; an appellate court has the power to review the judgment of a lower court (trial court) or tribunal. For example, the U.S. circuit courts of appeals review the decisions of the U.S. district courts.

Appellee	The party who opposes an appellant's appeal, and who seeks to persuade the appeals court to affirm the district court's decision.
Arraignment	A proceeding in which a criminal defendant is brought into court, told of the charges in an indictment or information, and asked to plead guilty or not guilty.
Article III judge	A federal judge who is appointed for life, during "good behavior," under Article III of the Constitution. Article III judges are nominated by the President and confirmed by the Senate.
Assets	Property of all kinds, including real and personal, tangible and intangible.
Assume	An agreement to continue performing duties under a contract or lease.
Automatic stay	An injunction that automatically stops lawsuits, foreclosures, garnishments, and most collection activities against the debtor the moment a bankruptcy petition is filed.

Go to top

B

Bail	The release, prior to trial, of a person accused of a crime, under specified conditions designed to assure that person's appearance in court when required. Also, can refer to the amount of bond money posted as a financial condition of pretrial release.
Bankruptcy	A legal procedure for dealing with debt problems of individuals and businesses; specifically, a case filed under one of the chapters of title 11 of the United States Code (the Bankruptcy Code).
Bankruptcy administrator	An officer of the Judiciary serving in the judicial districts of Alabama and North Carolina who, like the United States trustee, is responsible for supervising the administration of bankruptcy cases, estates, and trustees; monitoring plans and disclosure statements; monitoring creditors' committees; monitoring fee applications; and performing other statutory duties.
Bankruptcy code	The informal name for title 11 of the United States Code (11 U.S.C. §§ 101-1330), the federal bankruptcy law.
Bankruptcy court	The bankruptcy judges in regular active service in each

		district; a unit of the district court.
Bankruptcy estate		All interests of the debtor in property at the time of the bankruptcy filing. The estate technically becomes the temporary legal owner of all of the debtor's property.
Bankruptcy judge		A judicial officer of the United States district court who is the court official with decision-making power over federal bankruptcy cases.
Bankruptcy petition		A formal request for the protection of the federal bankruptcy laws. (There is an official form for bankruptcy petitions.)
Bankruptcy trustee		A private individual or corporation appointed in all Chapter 7 and Chapter 13 cases to represent the interests of the bankruptcy estate and the debtor's creditors.
Bench trial		A trial without a jury, in which the judge serves as the fact-finder.
Brief		A written statement submitted in a trial or appellate proceeding that explains one side's legal and factual arguments.

Burden of proof	The duty to prove disputed facts. In civil cases, a plaintiff generally has the burden of proving his or her case. In criminal cases, the government has the burden of proving the defendant's guilt. (See standard of proof.)
Business bankruptcy	A bankruptcy case in which the debtor is a business or an individual involved in business and the debts are for business purposes.

C

Capital offense	A crime punishable by death.
Case file	A complete collection of every document filed in court in a case.
Case law	The law as established in previous court decisions. A synonym for legal precedent. Akin to common law, which springs from tradition and judicial decisions.
Caseload	The number of cases handled by a judge or a court.
Cause of action	A legal claim.

Chambers	The offices of a judge and his or her staff.
Chapter 11	A reorganization bankruptcy, usually involving a corporation or partnership. A Chapter 11 debtor usually proposes a plan of reorganization to keep its business alive and pay creditors over time. Individuals or people in business can also seek relief in Chapter 11.
Chapter 12	The chapter of the Bankruptcy Code providing for adjustment of debts of a "family farmer" or "family fisherman," as the terms are defined in the Bankruptcy Code.
Chapter 13	The chapter of the Bankruptcy Code providing for the adjustment of debts of an individual with regular income, often referred to as a "wage-earner" plan. Chapter 13 allows a debtor to keep property and use his or her disposable income to pay debts over time, usually three to five years.
Chapter 13 trustee	A person appointed to administer a Chapter 13 case. A Chapter 13 trustee's responsibilities are similar to those of a Chapter 7 trustee; however, a Chapter 13 trustee has the additional responsibilities of overseeing the debtor's plan, receiving payments from debtors, and disbursing plan payments to creditors.

Chapter 15	The chapter of the Bankruptcy Code dealing with cases of cross-border insolvency.
Chapter 7	The chapter of the Bankruptcy Code providing for "liquidation," that is, the sale of a debtor's nonexempt property and the distribution of the proceeds to creditors. In order to be eligible for Chapter 7, the debtor must satisfy a "means test." The court will evaluate the debtor's income and expenses to determine if the debtor may proceed under Chapter 7.
Chapter 7 trustee	A person appointed in a Chapter 7 case to represent the interests of the bankruptcy estate and the creditors. The trustee's responsibilities include reviewing the debtor's petition and schedules, liquidating the property of the estate, and making distributions to creditors. The trustee may also bring actions against creditors or the debtor to recover property of the bankruptcy estate.
Chapter 9	The chapter of the Bankruptcy Code providing for reorganization of municipalities (which includes cities and towns, as well as villages, counties, taxing districts, municipal utilities, and school districts).
Chief judge	The judge who has primary responsibility for the administration of a court; chief judges are determined

	by seniority
Claim	A creditor's assertion of a right to payment from a debtor or the debtor's property.
Class action	A lawsuit in which one or more members of a large group, or class, of individuals or other entities sue on behalf of the entire class. The district court must find that the claims of the class members contain questions of law or fact in common before the lawsuit can proceed as a class action.
Clerk of court	The court officer who oversees administrative functions, especially managing the flow of cases through the court. The clerk's office is often called a court's central nervous system.
Collateral	Property that is promised as security for the satisfaction of a debt.
Common law	The legal system that originated in England and is now in use in the United States, which relies on the articulation of legal principles in a historical succession of judicial decisions. Common law principles can be changed by legislation.

Community service	A special condition the court imposes that requires an individual to work – without pay – for a civic or nonprofit organization.
Complaint	A written statement that begins a civil lawsuit, in which the plaintiff details the claims against the defendant.
Concurrent sentence	Prison terms for two or more offenses to be served at the same time, rather than one after the other. Example: Two five-year sentences and one three-year sentence, if served concurrently, result in a maximum of five years behind bars.
Confirmation	Approval of a plan of reorganization by a bankruptcy judge.
Consecutive sentence	Prison terms for two or more offenses to be served one after the other. Example: Two five-year sentences and one three-year sentence, if served consecutively, result in a maximum of 13 years behind bars.
Consumer bankruptcy	A bankruptcy case filed to reduce or eliminate debts that are primarily consumer debts.
Consumer debts	Debts incurred for personal, as opposed to business,

	needs.
Contingent claim	A claim that may be owed by the debtor under certain circumstances, e.g., where the debtor is a cosigner on another person's loan and that person fails to pay.
Contract	An agreement between two or more people that creates an obligation to do or not to do a particular thing.
Conviction	A judgment of guilt against a criminal defendant.
Counsel	Legal advice; a term also used to refer to the lawyers in a case.
Count	An allegation in an indictment or information, charging a defendant with a crime. An indictment or information may contain allegations that the defendant committed more than one crime. Each allegation is referred to as a count.
Court	Government entity authorized to resolve legal disputes. Judges sometimes use "court" to refer to themselves in the third person, as in "the court has read the briefs."
Court reporter	A person who makes a word-for-word record of what is

	said in court, generally by using a stenographic machine, shorthand or audio recording, and then produces a transcript of the proceedings upon request.
Credit counseling	Generally refers to two events in individual bankruptcy cases: (1) the "individual or group briefing" from a nonprofit budget and credit counseling agency that individual debtors must attend prior to filing under any chapter of the Bankruptcy Code; and (2) the "instructional course in personal financial management" in chapters 7 and 13 that an individual debtor must complete before a discharge is entered. There are exceptions to both requirements for certain categories of debtors, exigent circumstances, or if the U.S. trustee or bankruptcy administrator have determined that there are insufficient approved credit counseling agencies available to provide the necessary counseling.
Creditor	A person to whom or business to which the debtor owes money or that claims to be owed money by the debtor.
D	
Damages	Money that a defendant pays a plaintiff in a civil case if the plaintiff has won. Damages may be compensatory (for loss or injury) or punitive (to punish and deter future misconduct).

De facto	Latin, meaning "in fact" or "actually." Something that exists in fact but not as a matter of law.
De jure	Latin, meaning "in law." Something that exists by operation of law.
De novo	Latin, meaning "anew." A trial de novo is a completely new trial. Appellate review de novo implies no deference to the trial judge's ruling.
Debtor	A person who has filed a petition for relief under the Bankruptcy Code.
Debtor's plan	A debtor's detailed description of how the debtor proposes to pay creditors' claims over a fixed period of time.
Declaratory judgment	A judge's statement about someone's rights. For example, a plaintiff may seek a declaratory judgment that a particular statute, as written, violates some constitutional right.
Default judgment	A judgment awarding a plaintiff the relief sought in the complaint because the defendant has failed to

	appear in court or otherwise respond to the complaint.
Defendant	An individual (or business) against whom a lawsuit is filed.
Defendant	In a civil case, the person or organization against whom the plaintiff brings suit; in a criminal case, the person accused of the crime.
Deposition	An oral statement made before an officer authorized by law to administer oaths. Such statements are often taken to examine potential witnesses, to obtain discovery, or to be used later in trial. See discovery.
Discharge	A release of a debtor from personal liability for certain dischargeable debts. Notable exceptions to dischargeability are taxes and student loans. A discharge releases a debtor from personal liability for certain debts known as dischargeable debts and prevents the creditors owed those debts from taking any action against the debtor or the debtor's property to collect the debts. The discharge also prohibits creditors from communicating with the debtor regarding the debt, including through telephone calls, letters, and personal contact.
Dischargeable debt	A debt for which the Bankruptcy Code allows the

	debtor's personal liability to be eliminated.
Disclosure statement	A written document prepared by the chapter 11 debtor or other plan proponent that is designed to provide "adequate information" to creditors to enable them to evaluate the chapter 11 plan of reorganization.
Discovery	Procedures used to obtain disclosure of evidence before trial.
Dismissal with prejudice	Court action that prevents an identical lawsuit from being filed later.
Dismissal without prejudice	Court action that allows the later filing.
Disposable income	Income not reasonably necessary for the maintenance or support of the debtor or dependents. If the debtor operates a business, disposable income is defined as those amounts over and above what is necessary for the payment of ordinary operating expenses.
Docket	A log containing the complete history of each case in the form of brief chronological entries summarizing the court proceedings.

Due process	In criminal law, the constitutional guarantee that a defendant will receive a fair and impartial trial. In civil law, the legal rights of someone who confronts an adverse action threatening liberty or property.

E

En banc	French, meaning "on the bench." All judges of an appellate court sitting together to hear a case, as opposed to the routine disposition by panels of three judges. In the Ninth Circuit, an en banc panel consists of 11 randomly selected judges.
Equitable	Pertaining to civil suits in "equity" rather than in "law." In English legal history, the courts of "law" could order the payment of damages and could afford no other remedy (see damages). A separate court of "equity" could order someone to do something or to cease to do something (e.g., injunction). In American jurisprudence, the federal courts have both legal and equitable power, but the distinction is still an important one. For example, a trial by jury is normally available in "law" cases but not in "equity" cases.
Equity	The value of a debtor's interest in property that remains after liens and other creditors' interests are considered. (Example: If a house valued at $60,000 is subject to a $30,000 mortgage, there is $30,000 of equity.)

Evidence	Information presented in testimony or in documents that is used to persuade the fact finder (judge or jury) to decide the case in favor of one side or the other.
Ex parte	A proceeding brought before a court by one party only, without notice to or challenge by the other side.
Exclusionary rule	Doctrine that says evidence obtained in violation of a criminal defendant's constitutional or statutory rights is not admissible at trial.
Exculpatory evidence	Evidence indicating that a defendant did not commit the crime.
Executory contracts	Contracts or leases under which both parties to the agreement have duties remaining to be performed. If a contract or lease is executory, a debtor may assume it (keep the contract) or reject it (terminate the contract).
Exempt assets	Property that a debtor is allowed to retain, free from the claims of creditors who do not have liens on the property.
Exemptions, exempt property	Certain property owned by an individual debtor that the Bankruptcy Code or applicable state law permits the

	debtor to keep from unsecured creditors. For example, in some states the debtor may be able to exempt all or a portion of the equity in the debtor's primary residence (homestead exemption), or some or all "tools of the trade" used by the debtor to make a living (i.e., auto tools for an auto mechanic or dental tools for a dentist). The availability and amount of property the debtor may exempt depends on the state the debtor lives in.

F

Face sheet filing	A bankruptcy case filed either without schedules or with incomplete schedules listing few creditors and debts. (Face sheet filings are often made for the purpose of delaying an eviction or foreclosure
Family farmer	An individual, individual and spouse, corporation, or partnership engaged in a farming operation that meets certain debt limits and other statutory criteria for filing a petition under Chapter 12.
Federal public defender	An attorney employed by the federal courts on a full-time basis to provide legal defense to defendants who are unable to afford counsel. The judiciary administers the federal defender program pursuant to

	the Criminal Justice Act.
Federal public defender organization	As provided for in the Criminal Justice Act, an organization established within a federal judicial circuit to represent criminal defendants who cannot afford an adequate defense. Each organization is supervised by a federal public defender appointed by the court of appeals for the circuit.
Federal question jurisdiction	Jurisdiction given to federal courts in cases involving the interpretation and application of the U.S. Constitution, acts of Congress, and treaties.
Felony	A serious crime, usually punishable by at least one year in prison.
File	To place a paper in the official custody of the clerk of court to enter into the files or records of a case.
Fraudulent transfer	A transfer of a debtor's property made with intent to defraud or for which the debtor receives less than the transferred property's value.
Fresh start	The characterization of a debtor's status after bankruptcy, i.e., free of most debts. (Giving debtors a

	fresh start is one purpose of the Bankruptcy Code.)

G

Grand jury	A body of 16-23 citizens who listen to evidence of criminal allegations, which is presented by the prosecutors, and determine whether there is probable cause to believe an individual committed an offense. See also indictment and U.S. attorney.

H

Habeas corpus	Latin, meaning "you have the body." A writ of habeas corpus generally is a judicial order forcing law enforcement authorities to produce a prisoner they are holding, and to justify the prisoner's continued confinement. Federal judges receive petitions for a writ of habeas corpus from state prison inmates who say

	their state prosecutions violated federally protected rights in some way.
Hearsay	Evidence presented by a witness who did not see or hear the incident in question but heard about it from someone else. With some exceptions, hearsay generally is not admissible as evidence at trial
Home confinement	A special condition the court imposes that requires an individual to remain at home except for certain approved activities such as work and medical appointments. Home confinement may include the use of electronic monitoring equipment – a transmitter attached to the wrist or the ankle – to help ensure that the person stays at home as required.

Impeachment	1. The process of calling a witness's testimony into doubt. For example, if the attorney can show that the witness may have fabricated portions of his testimony, the witness is said to be "impeached;" 2. The constitutional process whereby the House of Representatives may "impeach" (accuse of misconduct) high officers of the federal government, who are then tried by the Senate.
In camera	Latin, meaning in a judge's chambers. Often means outside the presence of a jury and the public. In

	private.
In forma pauperis	"In the manner of a pauper." Permission given by the court to a person to file a case without payment of the required court fees because the person cannot pay them.
Inculpatory evidence	Evidence indicating that a defendant did commit the crime.
Indictment	The formal charge issued by a grand jury stating that there is enough evidence that the defendant committed the crime to justify having a trial; it is used primarily for felonies. See also information.
Information	A formal accusation by a government attorney that the defendant committed a misdemeanor. See also indictment.
Injunction	A court order preventing one or more named parties from taking some action. A preliminary injunction often is issued to allow fact-finding, so a judge can determine whether a permanent injunction is justified.
Insider (of corporate	A director, officer, or person in control of the debtor;

debtor)	a partnership in which the debtor is a general partner; a general partner of the debtor; or a relative of a general partner, director, officer, or person in control of the debtor.
Insider (of individual debtor)	Any relative of the debtor or of a general partner of the debtor; partnership in which the debtor is a general partner; general partner of the debtor; or corporation of which the debtor is a director, officer, or person in control.
Interrogatories	A form of discovery consisting of written questions to be answered in writing and under oath.
Issue	1. The disputed point between parties in a lawsuit; 2. To send out officially, as in a court issuing an order.

J

Joint administration	A court-approved mechanism under which two or more cases can be administered together. (Assuming no conflicts of interest, these separate businesses or individuals can pool their resources, hire the same professionals, etc.)
Joint petition	One bankruptcy petition filed by a husband and wife together.

Judge	An official of the Judicial branch with authority to decide lawsuits brought before courts. Used generically, the term judge may also refer to all judicial officers, including Supreme Court justices.
Judgeship	The position of judge. By statute, Congress authorizes the number of judgeships for each district and appellate court.
Judgment	The official decision of a court finally resolving the dispute between the parties to the lawsuit.
Judicial Conference of the United States	The policy-making entity for the federal court system. A 27-judge body whose presiding officer is the Chief Justice of the United States.
Jurisdiction	The legal authority of a court to hear and decide a certain type of case. It also is used as a synonym for venue, meaning the geographic area over which the court has territorial jurisdiction to decide cases.
Jurisprudence	The study of law and the structure of the legal system
Jury	The group of persons selected to hear the evidence

	in a trial and render a verdict on matters of fact. See also grand jury.
Jury instructions	A judge's directions to the jury before it begins deliberations regarding the factual questions it must answer and the legal rules that it must apply.

L

Lawsuit	A legal action started by a plaintiff against a defendant based on a complaint that the defendant failed to perform a legal duty which resulted in harm to the plaintiff.
Lien	A charge on specific property that is designed to secure payment of a debt or performance of an obligation. A debtor may still be responsible for a lien after a discharge.
Liquidated claim	A creditor's claim for a fixed amount of money.
Liquidation	The sale of a debtor's property with the proceeds to be used for the benefit of creditors.
Litigation	A case, controversy, or lawsuit. Participants (plaintiffs and defendants) in lawsuits are called litigants.

M

Magistrate judge	A judicial officer of a district court who conducts initial proceedings in criminal cases, decides criminal misdemeanor cases, conducts many pretrial civil and criminal matters on behalf of district judges, and decides civil cases with the consent of the parties.
Means test	Section 707(b)(2) of the Bankruptcy Code applies a "means test" to determine whether an individual debtor's chapter 7 filing is presumed to be an abuse of the Bankruptcy Code requiring dismissal or conversion of the case (generally to chapter 13). Abuse is presumed if the debtor's aggregate current monthly income (see definition above) over 5 years, net of certain statutorily allowed expenses is more than (i) $10,000, or (ii) 25% of the debtor's nonpriority unsecured debt, as long as that amount is at least $6,000. The debtor may rebut a presumption of abuse only by a showing of special circumstances that justify additional expenses or adjustments of current monthly income.
Mental health treatment	Special condition the court imposes to require an individual to undergo evaluation and treatment for a mental disorder. Treatment may include psychiatric,

	psychological, and sex offense-specific evaluations, inpatient or outpatient counseling, and medication.
Misdemeanor	An offense punishable by one year of imprisonment or less. See also felony.
Mistrial	An invalid trial, caused by fundamental error. When a mistrial is declared, the trial must start again with the selection of a new jury.
Moot	Not subject to a court ruling because the controversy has not actually arisen, or has ended
Motion	A request by a litigant to a judge for a decision on an issue relating to the case.
Motion in Limine	A pretrial motion requesting the court to prohibit the other side from presenting, or even referring to, evidence on matters said to be so highly prejudicial that no steps taken by the judge can prevent the jury from being unduly influenced.
Motion to lift the automatic stay	A request by a creditor to allow the creditor to take action against the debtor or the debtor's property that would otherwise be prohibited by the automatic stay.

N

No-asset case	A Chapter 7 case in which there are no assets available to satisfy any portion of the creditors' unsecured claims.
Nolo contendere	No contest. A plea of nolo contendere has the same effect as a plea of guilty, as far as the criminal sentence is concerned, but may not be considered as an admission of guilt for any other purpose.
Nondischargeable debt	A debt that cannot be eliminated in bankruptcy. Examples include a home mortgage, debts for alimony or child support, certain taxes, debts for most government funded or guaranteed educational loans or benefit overpayments, debts arising from death or personal injury caused by driving while intoxicated or under the influence of drugs, and debts for restitution or a criminal fine included in a sentence on the debtor's conviction of a crime. Some debts, such as debts for money or property obtained by false pretenses and debts for fraud or defalcation while acting in a fiduciary capacity may be declared nondischargeable only if a creditor timely files and prevails in a nondischargeability action.
Nonexempt assets	Property of a debtor that can be liquidated to satisfy

	claims of creditors.

O

Objection to dischargeability	A trustee's or creditor's objection to the debtor being released from personal liability for certain dischargeable debts. Common reasons include allegations that the debt to be discharged was incurred by false pretenses or that debt arose because of the debtor's fraud while acting as a fiduciary.
Objection to exemptions	A trustee's or creditor's objection to the debtor's attempt to claim certain property as exempt from liquidation by the trustee to creditors.
Opinion	A judge's written explanation of the decision of the court. Because a case may be heard by three or more judges in the court of appeals, the opinion in appellate decisions can take several forms. If all the judges completely agree on the result, one judge will write the opinion for all. If all the judges do not agree, the formal decision will be based upon the view of the majority, and one member of the majority will write the opinion. The judges who did not agree with the majority may write separately in dissenting or concurring opinions to present their views. A dissenting opinion disagrees with the majority opinion because of the reasoning and/or the principles of law the majority used to decide the

	case. A concurring opinion agrees with the decision of the majority opinion, but offers further comment or clarification or even an entirely different reason for reaching the same result. Only the majority opinion can serve as binding precedent in future cases. See also precedent.
Oral argument	An opportunity for lawyers to summarize their position before the court and also to answer the judges' questions.

P

Panel	1. In appellate cases, a group of judges (usually three) assigned to decide the case; 2. In the jury selection process, the group of potential jurors; 3. The list of attorneys who are both available and qualified to serve as court-appointed counsel for criminal defendants who cannot afford their own counsel.
Parole	The release of a prison inmate – granted by the U.S. Parole Commission – after the inmate has completed part of his or her sentence in a federal prison. When the parolee is released to

	the community, he or she is placed under the supervision of a U.S. probation officer.
The Sentencing Reform Act of 1984 abolished parole in favor of a determinate sentencing system in which the sentence is set by sentencing guidelines. Now, without the option of parole, the term of imprisonment the court imposes is the actual time the person spends in prison.	Party in interest
A party who has standing to be heard by the court in a matter to be decided in the bankruptcy case. The debtor, U.S. trustee or bankruptcy administrator, case trustee, and creditors are parties in interest for most matters.	Per curiam
Latin, meaning "for the court." In appellate courts, often refers to an unsigned opinion.	Peremptory challenge
A district court may grant each side in a civil or criminal trial the right	Petit jury (or trial jury)

to exclude a certain number of prospective jurors without cause or giving a reason.	
A group of citizens who hear the evidence presented by both sides at trial and determine the facts in dispute. Federal criminal juries consist of 12 persons. Federal civil juries consist of at least six persons.	Petition
The document that initiates the filing of a bankruptcy proceeding, setting forth basic information regarding the debtor, including name, address, chapter under which the case is filed, and estimated amount of assets and liabilities.	Petition preparer
A business not authorized to practice law that prepares bankruptcy petitions.	Petty offense
A federal misdemeanor punishable by six months or less in prison.	Plaintiff
A person or business that files a	Plan

formal complaint with the court.	
A debtor's detailed description of how the debtor proposes to pay creditors' claims over a fixed period of time.	Plea
In a criminal case, the defendant's statement pleading "guilty" or "not guilty" in answer to the charges. See also nolo contendere.	Pleadings
Written statements filed with the court that describe a party's legal or factual assertions about the case.	Postpetition transfer
A transfer of the debtor's property made after the commencement of the case.	Prebankruptcy planning
The arrangement (or rearrangement) of a debtor's property to allow the debtor to take maximum advantage of exemptions. (Prebankruptcy planning typically includes converting nonexempt assets into	Precedent

exempt assets.)	
A court decision in an earlier case with facts and legal issues similar to a dispute currently before a court. Judges will generally "follow precedent" - meaning that they use the principles established in earlier cases to decide new cases that have similar facts and raise similar legal issues. A judge will disregard precedent if a party can show that the earlier case was wrongly decided, or that it differed in some significant way from the current case.	Preferential debt payment
A debt payment made to a creditor in the 90-day period before a debtor files bankruptcy (or within one year if the creditor was an insider) that gives the creditor more than the creditor would receive in the debtor's chapter 7 case.	Presentence report
A report prepared by a court's probation officer, after a person has been convicted of an offense, summarizing for the court the background information needed to	Pretrial conference

determine the appropriate sentence.	
A meeting of the judge and lawyers to plan the trial, to discuss which matters should be presented to the jury, to review proposed evidence and witnesses, and to set a trial schedule. Typically, the judge and the parties also discuss the possibility of settlement of the case.	Pretrial services
A function of the federal courts that takes place at the very start of the criminal justice process – after a person has been arrested and charged with a federal crime and before he or she goes to trial. Pretrial services officers focus on investigating the backgrounds of these persons to help the court determine whether to release or detain them while they await trial. The decision is based on whether these individuals are likely to flee or pose a threat to the community. If the court orders release, a pretrial services officer supervises the person in the community until he or she returns to court.	Priority

The Bankruptcy Code's statutory ranking of unsecured claims that determines the order in which unsecured claims will be paid if there is not enough money to pay all unsecured claims in full.	Priority claim
An unsecured claim that is entitled to be paid ahead of other unsecured claims that are not entitled to priority status. Priority refers to the order in which these unsecured claims are to be paid.	Pro per
A slang expression sometimes used to refer to a pro se litigant. It is a corruption of the Latin phrase "in propria persona."	Pro se
Representing oneself. Serving as one's own lawyer.	Pro tem
Temporary.	Probation
Sentencing option in the federal courts. With probation, instead of	Probation officer

sending an individual to prison, the court releases the person to the community and orders him or her to complete a period of supervision monitored by a U.S. probation officer and to abide by certain conditions.	
Officers of the probation office of a court. Probation officer duties include conducting presentence investigations, preparing presentence reports on convicted defendants, and supervising released defendants.	Procedure
The rules for conducting a lawsuit; there are rules of civil procedure, criminal procedure, evidence, bankruptcy, and appellate procedure.	Proof of claim
A written statement describing the reason a debtor owes a creditor money, which typically sets forth the amount of money owed. (There is an official form for this purpose.)	Property of the estate

	Prosecute
All legal or equitable interests of the debtor in property as of the commencement of the case.	
To charge someone with a crime. A prosecutor tries a criminal case on behalf of the government	

R

Reaffirmation agreement	An agreement by a debtor to continue paying a dischargeable debt after the bankruptcy, usually for the purpose of keeping collateral or mortgaged property that would otherwise be subject to repossession.
Record	A written account of the proceedings in a case, including all pleadings, evidence, and exhibits submitted in the course of the case.
Redemption	A procedure in a Chapter 7 case whereby a debtor removes a secured creditor's lien on collateral by paying the creditor the value of the property. The debtor may then retain the property.
Remand	Send back.

Reverse	The act of a court setting aside the decision of a lower court. A reversal is often accompanied by a remand to the lower court for further proceedings.

S

Sanction	A penalty or other type of enforcement used to bring about compliance with the law or with rules and regulations.
Schedules	Lists submitted by the debtor along with the petition (or shortly thereafter) showing the debtor's assets, liabilities, and other financial information. (There are official forms a debtor must use.)
Secured creditor	A secured creditor is an individual or business that holds a claim against the debtor that is secured by a lien on property of the estate. The property subject to the lien is the secured creditor's collateral.
Secured debt	Debt backed by a mortgage, pledge of collateral, or other lien; debt for which the creditor has the right to pursue specific pledged property upon default. Examples include home mortgages, auto loans and tax

	liens.
Senior judge	A federal judge who, after attaining the requisite age and length of judicial experience, takes senior status, thus creating a vacancy among a court's active judges. A senior judge retains the judicial office and may cut back his or her workload by as much as 75 percent, but many opt to keep a larger caseload.
Sentence	The punishment ordered by a court for a defendant convicted of a crime.
Sentencing guidelines	A set of rules and principles established by the United States Sentencing Commission that trial judges use to determine the sentence for a convicted defendant.
Sequester	To separate. Sometimes juries are sequestered from outside influences during their deliberations.
Service of process	The delivery of writs or summonses to the appropriate party.
Settlement	Parties to a lawsuit resolve their dispute without having a trial. Settlements often involve the payment of compensation by one party in at least partial satisfaction of the other party's claims, but usually do

	not include the admission of fault.
Small business case	A special type of chapter 11 case in which there is no creditors' committee (or the creditors' committee is deemed inactive by the court) and in which the debtor is subject to more oversight by the U.S. trustee than other chapter 11 debtors. The Bankruptcy Code contains certain provisions designed to reduce the time a small business debtor is in bankruptcy.
Standard of proof	Degree of proof required. In criminal cases, prosecutors must prove a defendant's guilt "beyond a reasonable doubt." The majority of civil lawsuits require proof "by a preponderance of the evidence" (50 percent plus), but in some the standard is higher and requires "clear and convincing" proof.
Statement of financial affairs	A series of questions the debtor must answer in writing concerning sources of income, transfers of property, lawsuits by creditors, etc. (There is an official form a debtor must use.)
Statement of intention	A declaration made by a chapter 7 debtor concerning plans for dealing with consumer debts that are secured by property of the estate.

Statute	A law passed by a legislature.
Statute of limitations	The time within which a lawsuit must be filed or a criminal prosecution begun. The deadline can vary, depending on the type of civil case or the crime charged.
Sua sponte	Latin, meaning "of its own will." Often refers to a court taking an action in a case without being asked to do so by either side.
Subordination	The act or process by which a person's rights or claims are ranked below those of others.
Subpoena	A command, issued under a court's authority, to a witness to appear and give testimony.
Subpoena duces tecum	A command to a witness to appear and produce documents.

T

Temporary restraining order	Akin to a preliminary injunction, it is a judge's short-term order

	forbidding certain actions until a full hearing can be conducted. Often referred to as a TRO.
Testimony	Evidence presented orally by witnesses during trials or before grand juries.
Toll	See statute of limitations.
Tort	A civil, not criminal, wrong. A negligent or intentional injury against a person or property, with the exception of breach of contract.
Transcript	A written, word-for-word record of what was said, either in a proceeding such as a trial, or during some other formal conversation, such as a hearing or oral deposition
Transfer	Any mode or means by which a debtor disposes of or parts with his/her property.

Trustee	The representative of the bankruptcy estate who exercises statutory powers, principally for the benefit of the unsecured creditors, under the general supervision of the court and the direct supervision of the U.S. trustee or bankruptcy administrator. The trustee is a private individual or corporation appointed in all chapter 7, chapter 12, and chapter 13 cases and some chapter 11 cases. The trustee's responsibilities include reviewing the debtor's petition and schedules and bringing actions against creditors or the debtor to recover property of the bankruptcy estate. In chapter 7, the trustee liquidates property of the estate, and makes distributions to creditors. Trustees in chapter 12 and 13 have similar duties to a chapter 7 trustee and the additional responsibilities of overseeing the debtor's plan, receiving payments from debtors, and disbursing plan payments to creditors.
Typing service	A business not authorized to practice law that prepares

	bankruptcy petitions.
U	
U.S. attorney	A lawyer appointed by the President in each judicial district to prosecute and defend cases for the federal government. The U.S. Attorney employs a staff of Assistant U.S. Attorneys who appear as the government's attorneys in individual cases.
U.S. trustee	An officer of the U.S. Department of Justice responsible for supervising the administration of bankruptcy cases, estates, and trustees; monitoring plans and disclosure statements; monitoring creditors' committees; monitoring fee applications; and performing other statutory duties.
Undersecured claim	A debt secured by property that is worth less than the amount of the debt.
Undue hardship	The most widely used test for evaluating undue hardship in the

	dischargeability of a student loan includes three conditions: (1) the debtor cannot maintain – based on current income and expenses – a minimal standard of living if forced to repay the loans; (2) there are indications that the state of affairs is likely to persist for a significant portion of the repayment period; and (3) the debtor made good faith efforts to repay the loans.
Unlawful detainer action	A lawsuit brought by a landlord against a tenant to evict the tenant from rental property – usually for nonpayment of rent.
Unliquidated claim	A claim for which a specific value has not been determined.
Unscheduled debt	A debt that should have been listed by the debtor in the schedules filed with the court but was not. (Depending on the circumstances, an unscheduled debt may or may not be discharged.)

Unsecured claim	A claim or debt for which a creditor holds no special assurance of payment, such as a mortgage or lien; a debt for which credit was extended based solely upon the creditor's assessment of the debtor's future ability to pay.
Uphold	The appellate court agrees with the lower court decision and allows it to stand. See affirmed.

V

Venue	The geographic area in which a court has jurisdiction. A change of venue is a change or transfer of a case from one judicial district to another.
Verdict	The decision of a trial jury or a judge that determines the guilt or innocence of a criminal defendant, or that determines the final outcome of a civil case.
Voir dire	Jury selection process of questioning prospective jurors, to

	ascertain their qualifications and determine any basis for challenge.
Voluntary transfer	A transfer of a debtor's property with the debtor's consent.

W

Wage garnishment	A nonbankruptcy legal proceeding whereby a plaintiff or creditor seeks to subject to his or her claim the future wages of a debtor. In other words, the creditor seeks to have part of the debtor's future wages paid to the creditor for a debt owed to the creditor.
Warrant	Court authorization, most often for law enforcement officers, to conduct a search or make an arrest.
Witness	A person called upon by either side in a lawsuit to give testimony before the court or jury.
Writ	A written court order directing a person to take, or refrain from

	taking, a certain act.
Writ of certiorari	An order issued by the U.S. Supreme Court directing the lower court to transmit records for a case which it will hear on appeal.

Where to Proceed Next

Now that we've laid the foundation of legal terminology and explored the basics of law, governance, and the role of the state, you're equipped to dig deeper into more specialized areas of law. Here are some key areas to explore and the next steps in your journey to expand your legal knowledge.

1. State-Specific Laws

Laws can vary significantly between jurisdictions. To truly understand how the legal principles we've discussed apply to your life or business, it's essential to study your state's laws. These laws will guide you on issues ranging from criminal offenses, taxation, and business regulation, to civil rights and contracts.

Recommended Action:

- Start by visiting your state's official government website to access legislative texts and summaries.
- Look up statutes, regulations, and case law relevant to your specific interest areas, such as employment law or real estate law.
- Make use of **legal databases** like Westlaw or LexisNexis, which provide comprehensive case law and state statutes.

2. Intellectual Property (IP) Law

If you're interested in creativity, innovation, or business, learning about intellectual property (IP) law is essential. IP law protects the creations of the mind—such as inventions, literary works, and artistic designs—while balancing the interests of creators and the public.

What to Explore:
- *Copyright*: Protects original works of authorship, including books, music, and software.
- *Patents:* Provides protection for new inventions.
- **Trademarks**: Covers brand identity, including logos, slogans, and trade names.

Recommended Action:
- Familiarize yourself with the U.S. Patent and Trademark Office (USPTO) resources.
- Explore how international IP laws, such as the **Berne Convention** for copyright, impact global business.

3. International Law

International law governs the relationships between nations, covering topics like trade, war, human rights, and the environment. If you're interested in diplomacy, global business, or cross-border litigation, international law is a key field to understand.

What to Explore:

- Treaties: Agreements between nations, often facilitated by international organizations like the United Nations.

- Customary International Law: Unwritten laws that nations observe as binding, such as principles related to diplomatic immunity.

- International Trade Law: Governs trade agreements and disputes, such as those handled by the World Trade Organization (WTO).

Recommended Action:

- Study prominent international treaties and conventions, such as the **Geneva Conventions** or the **Paris Agreement**.

- Learn about organizations that enforce international law, like the **International Court of Justice (ICJ)** and the **International Criminal Court (ICC)**.

4. Legal Philosophy and Principles

Law is not just about rules and statutes; it's also about the underlying principles that give these laws meaning. Legal philosophy helps us question why laws exist, how justice is defined, and how society should be governed.

What to Explore:

- **Natural Law:** The idea that certain rights are inherent by virtue of human nature and can be understood universally through reason.

- **Legal Positivism:** Holds that law is a set of rules created by human authorities, not necessarily tied to morality.

- **The Rule of Law**: A principle that law should govern a nation, as opposed to being governed by arbitrary decisions of individual government officials.

Recommended Action:

- Read works by **John Locke**, **Thomas Hobbes**, or **H.L.A. Hart** to understand different schools of legal thought.
- Explore modern debates in legal philosophy, such as the balance between individual rights and public safety.

5. Uncovered Topics

While this guide has covered a broad range of subjects, there are still many areas of law we haven't touched on in depth. Here are some you may want to explore further:

- **Environmental Law**: Laws that regulate the interaction between humans and the natural environment.
- **Labor Law**: Governs the relationship between employers, employees, and trade unions.
- **Family Law**: Covers issues like marriage, divorce, and child custody.
- **Bankruptcy Law**: Focuses on the process for businesses or individuals who are unable to repay their debts.

Recommended Action:

- Visit legal information websites such as **Justia** or **NOLO** for introductory articles on these subjects.
- Attend webinars or take online courses on specific legal topics you're interested in.

By continuing to explore these areas, you will deepen your understanding of the legal landscape and be better equipped to apply the law to your personal or professional life. Stay curious and always remember that the law is a living field, constantly evolving with society. Keep up-to-date with changes and engage with legal materials to continue your legal education!

When You Must Consult a Lawyer: Specific Cases and General Guidelines

While this guide aims to provide a foundational understanding of various legal concepts, there are numerous situations where consulting a licensed lawyer is not just advisable but essential. Legal professionals are trained to navigate complex statutes, case law, and procedural rules to ensure your rights are protected and your interests are represented. Below are key scenarios where seeking legal counsel is crucial:

1. Contract Drafting and Review

Whenever you're dealing with significant agreements—such as employment contracts, business deals, or lease agreements—consulting a lawyer is a wise step. A lawyer can:

- Ensure that the terms are in your favor or, at the very least, fair.
- Point out any hidden clauses or legal jargon that could create future problems.
- Help you avoid pitfalls in poorly written or misleading agreements, especially in high-stakes areas like **franchise contracts** or **investment deals**.

Common Contracts to Have a Lawyer Review:

- Employment contracts (particularly with non-compete or NDA clauses).
- Franchise agreements.
- Real estate leases or purchase agreements.
- Business partnership agreements.

2. Complex Business Transactions

Starting a business is exciting but involves many legal intricacies. Lawyers are vital for:

- **Forming a legal entity**: They help you choose between LLCs, corporations, partnerships, etc., ensuring that your liability and taxes are handled correctly.
- **Mergers and Acquisitions**: If you are buying or selling a business, the paperwork and due diligence can be overwhelming.
- **Intellectual Property Protection**: Registering patents, trademarks, and copyrights requires legal precision to protect your ideas.

General Advice: Avoid "template" contracts or online-only services for anything beyond basic, low-risk transactions. Custom legal advice ensures your specific needs are covered.

3. Lawsuits and Litigation

If you're involved in a lawsuit, whether as the plaintiff or defendant, hiring a lawyer is almost always essential. Courts have complex procedures that are difficult to navigate without expert knowledge, and the consequences of losing a case can be severe.

- **Personal injury claims**: If you've been injured in an accident, especially with long-term effects.
- **Business disputes**: Disagreements with partners, suppliers, or customers may require litigation or negotiation.
- **Criminal defense**: Any criminal charges require immediate consultation with a criminal lawyer to protect your rights.

4. Family Law Matters

Family-related legal issues are emotionally charged and often legally complex. Consult a lawyer for:

- Divorce proceedings: Issues around property division, child custody, and spousal support can be difficult to navigate without professional help.
- Adoption or child custody disputes.
- Domestic violence cases: Lawyers can help secure protection orders and provide advice on criminal charges.

5. Estate Planning

When it comes to planning your future, ensuring your wishes are legally enforceable is crucial. Lawyers can assist with:

- Drafting a will or living trust: This ensures your assets are distributed according to your wishes.

- Establishing powers of attorney: This can be critical for medical or financial decisions if you're incapacitated.
- Guardianship arrangements: If you have minor children, a lawyer can ensure their guardianship is legally binding.

6. Tax Matters

If you're dealing with complicated tax issues—whether personal or business—consulting a tax attorney is a smart move. Tax law is notoriously complicated and a single misstep can lead to significant financial penalties.

- **Business taxes**: Startups and corporations may need assistance understanding tax liabilities.
- **IRS audits**: If you're audited, having a lawyer can make a significant difference in navigating the process.

7. Immigration Issues

Immigration law is intricate and constantly changing. A lawyer can help ensure you're following the correct procedures, whether you're applying for a visa, green card, or citizenship.

8. Criminal Charges

If you are facing criminal charges, whether misdemeanor or felony, immediate legal advice is critical. Criminal lawyers are trained to protect your rights and help mitigate consequences.

- Even minor offenses can have lasting impacts on your record and future opportunities.

9. Disputes with Government or Administrative Agencies

Whether it's a zoning dispute, a regulatory issue, or a conflict with a government agency, legal advice is crucial. Administrative law can be complex, and a lawyer can help negotiate, file appeals, or take your case to court.

General Measures to Consider

- **Be Proactive**: Don't wait until something goes wrong to seek legal advice. Prevention is always better than damage control.
- **Document Everything**: Keep records of contracts, communications, and agreements. A well-documented paper trail can be crucial if legal issues arise later.
- **Know When You're Out of Depth**: If you encounter unfamiliar legal issues, it's usually a sign that you need professional guidance.

By consulting a lawyer in these scenarios, you not only protect your rights but often save time, money, and stress in the long run.

Copyright © 2024 by Ahmad A. Salahat

All rights reserved.
No part of this book may be reproduced, distributed, or transmitted in any form or by any means, including photocopying, recording, or other electronic or mechanical methods, without the prior written permission of the author, except in the case of brief quotations embodied in critical reviews and certain other non-commercial uses permitted by copyright law.

For permission requests, please contact the author at: [ahmad@a-salahat.me]

www.ingramcontent.com/pod-product-compliance
Lightning Source LLC
Chambersburg PA
CBHW052202220526
45471CB00004B/1771